Welcome!

Bringing home a new pu be one of the best day life. But you need to m sure that you are gettir of your dreams, rather than takir step into your worst nightmare.

Finding a dog to buy is easy - t end of dubious people keen to sell you a pup over the internet or in the free papers. But hopefully you'll read the next two pages and be aware that just as there are battery-farmed chickens, there's a similar sorry trade in dogs, which you really don't want any part of.

If you want to find the Perfect Pup, you need a plan...

✓ Get the right breed to fit your life
✓ From a really caring breeder or rescue
✓ Use errorless and kind training methods
✓ Put your name down for a good reward-based puppy class
✓ Get comprehensive health insurance, not just the cheapest
✓ Feed a quality food you believe in

This book aims to give you everything you need to get it right.

If you're still scratching your head after looking through all our breed profiles, you'll find a free lifestyle questionnaire at the back. Plus, there are some very useful vouchers and a great subscription offer for the most ethical dog magazine on the market.

Please do immediately insure your pup. Beware, pet insurance is not like car insurance - you can't compare premiums and just pick the cheapest. It will be like comparing apples and bananas. Very cheap insurance has so many exclusions that it'll be virtually useless. I've dealt with so many calls from distraught people who didn't read the small print when they opted for the lowest possible premium. There's no NHS for dogs.

Do look at our website www.perfectpup.co.uk or check out our monthly magazine *Dogs Today* for more help and advice. We carry information on litters for sale if we find breeders who have done all the health tests and who rear their pups in the home.

Good luck in finding your new best friend and I should just point out the obvious - that even the most perfect of pups can sometimes chew your shoes or pinch the Sunday roast!

Beverley Cuddy, *Editor*

Published in 2009 by Pet Subjects Ltd
Copyright Pet Subjects Limited 2009

First Published in Great Britain by:
Pet Subjects Ltd, The Dog House,
4 Bonseys Lane, Chobham,
Surrey, GU24 8JJ
Tel: 01276 858880

www.dogstodaymagazine.co.uk
www.perfectpup.co.uk

ISBN: 978-0-9563327-0-7

Photography by: Tim Rose @ Martin Dawe Photography unless otherwise stated.

Editor: Beverley Cuddy

Contributors: Dr Ian Dunbar, Robert Killick, Justine Hankins, John Burns, Gwen Bailey, Claire Horton-Bussey, Luke Warren, Karen Redpath, Christine Bailey and Chloé Addo

Designed by:
Rosie Peace, Appletree Design

Printed and bound by:
Cambrian Printers, Llanbadarn Road, Aberystwyth, Ceredigion, SY23 3TN

CW00485654

Buying a badly reared dog can break your heart - and the bank, says **Beverley Cuddy**. Follow our advice to find the perfect puppy and avoid battery-farmed pups...

As soon as you decide you'd like a puppy in your life, even the most grounded among us can be led astray. Such is the power that sweet little puppies have over us that - just the sight of a litter can turn our critical faculties to complete mush.

It is wise to avoid placing yourself in temptation's way at this extremely vulnerable time, as many before you have fallen prey to a deeply unwise impulse purchase.

Months of careful research can go out of the window when we catch the pitiful gaze of a pup obviously past its sell-by date for sale in a shady-looking pet shop. Buying a puppy out of pity is probably the very worst thing you can do, from every perspective.

For a start, most experts think puppies and kittens should never be sold by anyone other than breeders and rescue charities, but sadly our consumer laws don't yet prohibit it. People after a quick profit can simply buy cheap, poorly bred pups raised on ghastly battery puppy farms in Wales, Ireland, and elsewhere, and then resell these often sickly pups through pet shops, free newspapers and internet sites, making themselves a tidy profit.

These badly bred pups are more likely to have inherited diseases - that's if they survive long enough for these problems to reveal themselves. Puppy farmers aren't going to be eating into their profit margins by performing preventative health-screening tests or being too bothered about worming, de-fleaing or feeding the best diets.

Dealers will regularly pick up from lots of puppy farms, and, by combining litters from many sources, they make these pups vulnerable to cross-infection of deadly diseases like parvovirus. The stress of being taken from a ramshackle shed to a busy city-centre location can also take its toll on pups, making them much more prone to illness and behaviour problems.

In the 19 years I have been editing *Dogs Today* magazine, I have heard so many sad stories of intelligent people who fell for a pet-shop puppy and then had the misery of the poor thing dying at the vets after running up a massive medical bill.

Please don't allow this to happen to you. We have to break the chain and stop funding this miserable trade. If it isn't profitable, intensive puppy farming will stop. And if you salve your conscience by imagining you have 'saved' a pup by buying it from a shop, remember the poor dog's mum, who will never enjoy home comforts and is going to live a miserable life as a breeding slave, producing many more pups you can't save.

When you go shopping for all the exciting new things your puppy will need, please check you're going to shops that don't sell pups. The nation's biggest pet-store chain, Pets At Home, is definitely a safe haven.

So now you're up to speed on battery-farmed dogs, you hopefully want to hear about the best place to get a dog.

Most dog behaviour experts agree that a puppy should ideally be reared in a similar environment to the one it's going to end up living in. A litter reared in a busy home will already be used to people and household noises. A good breeder will have started housetraining your puppy long before you bring him or her home, and will be a constant source of help and advice for your pup's entire life.

In a dream world you want a breeder who is having pups for the love of their breed and is doing everything they can to make future generations as healthy as possible - and that means health screening in breeds with known problems and only breeding from dogs that have good temperaments.

These breeders are usually very fussy about who has their pups and you should expect to be asked lots of questions so they can be satisfied you are going to be a good owner. Being interrogated is a very good sign! If they care that much about their pup's future, you can be sure they've not scrimped on rearing. If the only question you are asked is, "How do you want to pay?" then leave the premises.

Another reason to walk away is if you can't see the dog's mother. Be highly suspicious if she is not present, as there could be a chance that you're dealing with a dealer, who has bought up these pups from a puppy farm. Also, if someone offers to deliver your puppy to your home or meet halfway at a service station, beware - this can be another dealer's trick to conceal the fact he or she doesn't own the mum. It's unusual to be able to see dad, too - so don't be spooked by that. Most good breeders will be using an unrelated stud dog rather than one of their own dogs.

Don't be overly impressed by pedigrees full of Champions unless you are thinking of taking up dog showing yourself. Be more impressed by health certificates that prove the breeder is doing everything possible to keep their breed healthy.

We have listed a few contacts of very knowledgeable people in every breed. They can introduce you to a network of caring breeders who usually don't have to advertise their pups for sale. Most good breeders will register their dogs with the Kennel Club, but sadly some very bad breeders also use their registration system - so don't imagine that it is in itself a mark of quality.

Breeders of Labradoodles and Cockerpoos cannot use the KC to register their pups, as their breeds are not recognised by the club. Again, there are good and bad breeders producing so-called 'designer dogs'; be very suspicious of anyone making false claims of their dogs being hypoallergenic. Breeders of first crosses should still be health testing their dogs for the hereditary problems of all the breeds involved. No matter the breed, breeders who health test are generally the most caring and knowledgeable. People breeding purely for money will not bother.

For every breed we've also included a breed-specific rescue contact. Many dogs end up homeless through no fault of their own - divorces and bereavement being the main factors. Nearly every breed has a band of wonderful volunteers who try to match dogs to new owners. Some breeds have very long waiting lists for rescues, so you'll need to be patient; others, such as Staffie, Border Collie and Rottie rescues, are really struggling to find enough homes and would dearly love more people to consider them.

These days your local rescue kennels will mainly be full of pedigree dogs looking for new homes. In fact, anyone trying to find a genuine mongrel will probably have the hardest search of all.

Good luck with your search and please, please, please stay away from temptation!

Be suspicious if...

✗ You can't see mum

✗ They offer to deliver

✗ If they don't grill you

✗ They don't do health tests

✗ The pups aren't reared in the home

Still not sure which breed is for you? Fill in the Plan-a-Pup form at the back of this book for free advice

In a dream world you want a breeder who is having pups for the love of their breed and is doing everything they can to make future generations as healthy as possible - and that means health screening in breeds with known problems and only breeding from dogs that have good temperaments

To get a safe, reliable adult dog, the key is not to *stop* him biting when he is a puppy, says **Dr Ian Dunbar** - but to show him *how* to bite!

Puppy biting is a normal, natural, and necessary puppy behaviour. Puppy play-biting is the means by which dogs develop bite inhibition and a soft mouth. The more your puppy bites and receives appropriate feedback, the safer his jaws will be in adulthood. It is the puppy that does not mouth and bite as a youngster whose adult bites are more likely to cause serious damage.

The developing puppy should learn that his bites can hurt long before he develops jaws strong enough to inflict injury. The greater the pup's opportunity to play-bite with people, other dogs, and other animals, the better his bite inhibition will be as an adult. For puppies that do not grow up with the benefit of regular interaction with other dogs and other animals, the responsibility of teaching bite inhibition lies totally with the owner.

Good bite inhibition is the most important quality of any companion dog. Moreover, a dog must develop bite inhibition during puppyhood, before he is four-and-a-half months old.

Good bite inhibition means that should the dog snap and lunge, his teeth will seldom make skin contact and should the dog's teeth ever make skin contact, the inhibited 'bite' will cause little, if any, damage.

No matter how well you try to socialise your dog, accidents happen:

- A friend of the owner unintentionally slammed a car door on a dog's tail.
- A woman wearing high heels unintentionally stepped on her sleeping Rottweiler's thigh.
- An owner grabbed his Jack Russell by the collar.
- A groomer was combing out a Wheaten's matted coat.
- A vet was fixing a Bernese Mountain Dog's dislocated elbow.
- A visitor tripped and flew headlong to butt heads with an Airedale chewing his bone.
- A three-year-old child wearing a Superman cape jumped from a coffee table and landed on the ribcage of a sleeping Malamute.

The Rottweiler and Bernese both screamed. The Bernese lay perfectly still and did not attempt to bite. All the other dogs grrrrwuffffed and quickly turned their muzzles towards the person. The Malamute got up and left the room. Both the Rottweiler and Jack Russell snapped and lunged, but neither made skin contact. The Wheaten took hold of the groomer's arm and squeezed gently. The Airedale nicked the visitor's cheek.

All of these dogs were pretty friendly most of the time, but what is crucially important is that they had all developed stellar bite inhibition in puppyhood. Despite extreme fright or pain, bite inhibition instantly clicked in to check the bite. Consequently, none of these dogs caused any damage.

The dog with the trapped tail mutilated the person's arm with multiple deep bites. This dog was a breed most people consider to be extremely friendly and had been taken on numerous visits to schools and hospitals. Indeed, the dog was extremely friendly, but she had no bite inhibition.

During puppyhood, she did not play with other dogs much, and her puppy biting behaviour was infrequent and gentle. Because the dog had never displayed any signs of unfriendliness as an adult, there was no warning that she might bite. And because she had never snapped or bitten before, there was no warning that her bite would be serious. For a dog that is likely to spend a lot of time around people, being well socialised but having poor bite inhibition is a dangerous combination.

Some people might feel that a dog is justified to bite in self-defence. But that is not what really happened in any of the above instances. In each case, the dog may have felt that he/she was under attack, but in reality the dog bit a person who had no intention of hurting him/her.

Whether you agree with this or not, the fact remains that we humans have been socialised not to attack our hairdressers, dentists, doctors, friends, and acquaintances when they unintentionally hurt us. Likewise, it is extremely easy, and essential, to train our dogs not to attack groomers, vets, family, friends, and visitors.

Gently does it

The first step is to stop your puppy from hurting people: to teach him to inhibit the force of his play-bites. It is not necessary to reprimand the pup, and certainly physical punishments are not called for. But it is essential to let your puppy know that bites can hurt.

A simple "Ouch!" is usually sufficient. When the puppy backs off, take a short time out to "lick your wounds," and instruct your pup to come, sit, and lie down to apologise and make up. Then resume playing. If your puppy does not respond to your yelp by easing up or backing off, an effective technique is to call the puppy a "Bully!" and then leave the room and shut the door.

Allow the pup a minute or two of time-out to reflect on the association between his painful bite and the immediate departure of his favourite human playmate. Then return to make up. It is important to show that you still love your puppy, only that his painful bites are objectionable. Have your pup come and sit and then resume playing once more.

It is much better for you to walk away from the pup than to physically restrain him or remove him to his confinement area at a time when he is biting too hard. So make a habit of playing with your puppy in his long-term confinement area. This technique is remarkably effective since it is precisely the way puppies learn to inhibit the force of their bites when playing with each other. If one puppy bites another too hard, the 'bitee' yelps and playing is postponed while he licks his wounds. The biter soon learns that hard bites interrupt an otherwise enjoyable play

session. He learns to bite more softly once play resumes.

The next step is to eliminate bite pressure entirely, even though the 'bites' no longer hurt. While your puppy is chewing his human chew-toy, wait for a bite that is harder than the rest and respond as if it really hurt, even though it didn't: "Ouch, you worm! Gennntly! That really hurt me, you bully!" Your puppy begins to think, "Good heavens! These humans are soooooo sensitive. I'll have to be really careful when mouthing their delicate skin." And that's precisely what you want your pup to think: that he needs to be extremely careful and gentle when playing with people.

Your pup should learn not to hurt people well before he is three months old. Ideally, by the time he is four-and-a-half months old - before he develops strong jaws and adult canine teeth - he should no longer be exerting any pressure when mouthing.

Don't touch

Once your puppy has been taught to mouth gently, it is time to reduce the frequency of mouthing. Your pup must learn that mouthing is okay, but he must stop when requested. Why? Because it is inconvenient to drink a cup of tea or to answer the telephone with 50 lbs of wriggling pup dangling from your wrist, that's why!

It is better to first teach "Off" using food as both a distraction and a reward. The deal is this: once I say "Off," if you don't touch the food treat in my hand

for just one second, I'll say, "Take it" and you can have it. Once your pup has mastered this simple task, up the ante to two or three seconds of non-contact, and then to five, eight, 12, 20, and so on. Count out the seconds and praise the dog with each second: "Good dog one, good dog two, good dog three," and so forth. If the pup touches the treat before you are ready to give it, simply start the count from zero again. Your pup quickly learns that once you say "Off," he cannot have the treat until he has not touched it, for, say, eight seconds, so the quickest way to get the treat is not to touch it for the first eight seconds. In addition, regular handfeeding during this exercise encourages your pup's soft mouth.

Once your pup understands the "Off" request, use food as a lure and a reward to teach it to let go when mouthing. Say, "Off" and waggle some food as a lure to entice your pup to let go and sit. Then praise the pup and give the food as a reward when he does so.

The main point of this exercise is to practise stopping the pup from mouthing, and so each time your puppy obediently ceases and desists, resume playing once more. Stop and start the session many times over. Also, since the puppy wants to mouth, the best reward for stopping mouthing is to allow him to mouth again. When you decide to stop the mouthing session altogether, say, "Off" and then offer your puppy a Kong stuffed with kibble.

The articles in this section are extracts from two books written by Dr Ian Dunbar. The full versions of *Before You Get Your Puppy* and *After You Get Your Puppy* are available free to download from www.dogstardaily .com

www.dogstardaily .com is a free website for dog lovers - a daily magazine with news, blogs, articles about dog behaviour, a comprehensive digital dog training textbook, plus a place to share photos and videos of your favourite canine companions

Want to know more?

Good bite inhibition is the most important quality of any companion dog. Moreover, a dog must develop bite inhibition during puppyhood, before he is four-and-a-half months old

Other puppies are the very best teachers. They say, "Bite me too hard and I'm not going to play with you anymore!"

Bite-size training

If ever your pup refuses to release your hand when requested, say, "Bully!" rapidly extricate your hand from his mouth, and storm out of the room mumbling, "Right. That's done it! You've ruined it! Finished! Over! No more!" and shut the door in his face. Give the pup a couple of minutes on his own to reflect on his loss and then go back to call him to come and sit and make up before continuing the mouthing game.

By the time your pup is five months old, he must have a mouth as soft as a 14-year-old working Labrador Retriever: your puppy should never initiate mouthing unless requested; he should never exert any pressure when mouthing; and he should stop mouthing and calm down immediately upon request by any family member.

Whether or not you allow your adult dog to mouth on request is up to you. For most owners, I recommend that they teach their dog to discontinue mouthing people altogether by the time he is six to eight months old. However, it is essential to continue bite inhibition exercises. Otherwise, your dog's bite will begin to drift and become harder as he grows older.

It is important to regularly handfeed your dog and clean his teeth each day, since these exercises involve a human hand in his mouth.

Don't stop biting
A common mistake is to punish the pup in an attempt to get him to stop biting. At best, the puppy no longer bites those family members who can effectively punish him but instead directs his biting toward those who have no control: for example, children. What is worse, because the pup does not mouth them, parents are often unaware of the child's plight.

Worse still, the puppy may no longer mouth people at all. Hence, he receives no training for inhibiting the force of his bites. All is fine until someone accidentally treads on the dog's foot, or shuts the car door on his tail, whereupon the dog bites and the bite punctures the skin because there has been insufficient bite inhibition.

Time for school
As soon as your puppy is three months old, there is an urgent need to play catch-up in terms of socialisation and confidence-building with other dogs. At the very latest, before he is 18 weeks old, your pup should start puppy training classes.

Four-and-a-half months marks a critical juncture in your dog's development, the point at which he changes from puppy to adolescent, sometimes virtually overnight. You certainly want to be enrolled in class before your pup collides with adolescence. I cannot overemphasise the importance of placing yourself under the guidance and tutelage of a professional pet dog trainer during your dog's difficult transition from puppyhood to adolescence.

Puppy classes allow your pup to develop canine social savvy while playing with other puppies in a non-threatening and controlled setting. Shy and fearful pups quickly gain confidence in leaps and bounds, and bullies learn to tone it down and be gentle.

Puppy play sessions are crucially important. Play is essential for pups to build confidence and learn canine social etiquette, so that later on as socialised adult dogs they would much rather play than either fight or take flight. If not sufficiently socialised as puppies, dogs generally lack the confidence to have fun and play as adults. Moreover, once they are fearful or aggressive as adults, dogs can be difficult to rehabilitate. Luckily, these potentially serious problems with adult dogs are easily prevented in puppyhood, simply by letting puppies play with each other. So give your puppy this opportunity. It's not fair to condemn your dog to a lifetime of social worry and anxiety by denying him the opportunity to play during puppyhood.

This is not to say that a socialised dog will never spook or scrap. A socialised dog may be momentarily startled, but he gets over it quickly. Unsocialised dogs do not. Also, socialised dogs, who have encountered all sizes and sorts of dogs, are better equipped to deal with occasional encounters with unsocialised or unfriendly dogs.

Bite school

The number-one reason for attending puppy class is to provide your puppy with the very best opportunity to fine-tune his bite inhibition. Whether your puppy is still biting you too much and harder than you would like, or whether he is biting less than necessary to develop reliable bite inhibition, puppy play sessions are the solution. Other puppies are the very best teachers. They say, "Bite me too hard and I'm not going to play with you anymore!" Since puppies want to spend all their time play-fighting and play-biting, they end up teaching other puppies bite-inhibition.

Classes of young puppies of about the same age generate high energy and activity levels, pretty much on par with groups of similar-aged children. Each puppy stimulates the others to give chase and play-fight, such that the frequency of bites during puppy play is astronomical. Moreover, each puppy tends to rev up all the others, such that the physical nature of the play and the force of play-bites periodically increase to the point where one puppy predictably bites another too hard and receives the appropriate feedback. A young puppy's skin is extremely sensitive, so pups are likely to provide immediate and convincing feedback when bitten too hard. In fact, a pup is likely to receive better feedback regarding the force of his bites during a single one-hour puppy class than he would all week from his owners at home.

Moreover, much of the pup's bite inhibition with other dogs will generalise to good bite inhibition with people, making the pup easier to train and control at home.

Now, as mentioned earlier, even well-socialised dogs may have occasional disagreements and squabbles. After all, who doesn't? But just as we have learned how to resolve disagreements with each other and with our dogs in a socially acceptable manner without tearing flesh or breaking bones, so can socialised dogs. Although it is unrealistic to expect dogs never to squabble and scrap, it is absolutely realistic to expect dogs to settle their differences without mutilating people or other dogs. It all depends on the level of bite inhibition they develop while mouthing other puppies in play. ●

Puppy play sessions are crucially important. Play is essential for pups to build confidence and learn canine social etiquette, so that later on as socialised adult dogs they would much rather play than either fight or take flight

Your canine newcomer is just itching to learn household manners, says **Dr Ian Dunbar**. She wants to please, but she has to learn how...

Errorless housetraining

Before the young pup can be trusted to have full run of the house, somebody must teach the house rules.

Without a firm grounding in canine domestic etiquette, your puppy will be left to improvise in her choice of toys and toilets. The pup will no doubt eliminate on carpets, and your couches and curtains will be viewed as mere playthings for destruction. Each mistake is a potential disaster, since it heralds many more to come. If your pup is allowed to make 'mistakes', bad habits will quickly become the status quo, making it necessary to break bad habits before teaching good ones.

Begin by teaching your puppy good habits from the very first day she comes home. Remember, good habits are just as hard to break as bad habits. Most pressing, your puppy's living quarters need to be designed so that housetraining and chew toy training are errorless.

Housesoiling is a spatial problem, involving perfectly normal, natural, and necessary canine behaviours (peeing and pooping) performed in inappropriate places.

Housetraining is quickly and easily accomplished by praising your puppy and offering a food treat when she eliminates in an appropriate toilet area. Once

- **To confine the puppy to an area where chewing and toilet behaviour is acceptable, so the puppy does not make any chewing or housesoiling mistakes around the house**

- **To maximize the likelihood that the puppy will learn to use the provided toilet, to chew only chewtoys (the only chewables available in the playroom), and to settle down calmly without barking.**

your pup realises that her eliminatory products are the equivalent of coins in a food vending machine - that faeces and urine may be cashed in for tasty treats - your pup will be clamouring to eliminate in the appropriate spot, because soiling the house does not bring equivalent fringe benefits.

Housesoiling is also a temporal problem: either the puppy is in the wrong place at the right time (confined indoors with full bladder and bowels), or the puppy is in the right place at the wrong time (outdoors in the yard or on a walk, but with empty bladder and bowels).

Timing is of the essence for successful housetraining. Indeed, efficient and effective housetraining depends upon the owner being able to predict when the puppy needs to eliminate so that she may be directed to an appropriate toilet area and more than adequately rewarded for doing the right thing in the right place at the right time.

Usually, puppies urinate within half a minute of waking up from a nap and usually defecate within a couple of minutes of that. But who has the time to hang around to wait for puppy to wake up and pee and poop? Instead it's a better plan to wake up the puppy yourself, when you are ready and the time is right.

Short-term confinement offers a convenient means to accurately predict when your puppy needs to relieve herself. Confining a pup to a small area strongly inhibits her from urinating or defecating, since she doesn't want to soil her sleeping area. Hence, the puppy is highly likely to want to eliminate immediately after being released from confinement.

When you can't be there

Keep your puppy confined to a fairly small puppy playroom, such as the kitchen, bathroom, or utility room. You can also use an exercise pen to cordon off a small section of a room. This is your puppy's long-stay confinement area.

It should include:
- A comfortable bed
- A water bowl with fresh water
- Six hollow chewtoys (stuffed with dog food)
- A doggie toilet in the farthest corner from her bed

Obviously, your puppy will feel the need to bark, chew, and eliminate if you need to leave her for a few hours, and so she must be left somewhere she can satisfy her needs without causing any damage or annoyance. Your puppy will most probably eliminate as far as possible from her sleeping quarters - in her doggie toilet. By removing all chewable items from the puppy playpen - with the exception of hollow chewtoys stuffed with kibble, you will make chewing chewtoys your puppy's favourite habit - a good habit! ▶

Without doubt, housesoiling and destructive chewing are the two most prevalent terminal illnesses in dogs. Using a dog crate will help you prevent these problems from ever developing in your puppy

When you are at home

Enjoy short play and training sessions hourly. If you cannot pay full attention, play with your pup in his puppy playpen, where a suitable toilet and toys are available. Or, for periods of no longer than an hour at a time, confine your puppy to his doggie den (short-stay close confinement area), such as a portable dog crate. Every hour, release your puppy and quickly take him to his doggie toilet.

Your puppy's short-term confinement area should include a comfortable bed and plenty of hollow chewtoys (stuffed with dog food).

It is much easier to watch your pup if he is settled down in a single spot. Either you may move the crate so that your puppy is in the same room as you, or you may want to confine your pup to a different room to start preparing him for times when he will be left at home alone. If you do not like the idea of confining your puppy to a dog crate, tie the leash to your belt and have the pup settle down at your feet.

- To confine the puppy to an area where chewing behaviour is acceptable so the puppy does not make chewing mistakes around the house

- To make the puppy a chewtoyaholic (since chewtoys are the only chewables available and they are stuffed with food) and to teach the puppy to settle down calmly and happily for periodic quiet moments

- To prevent housesoiling mistakes around the house and to predict when the puppy needs to eliminate. Dogs naturally avoid soiling their den, so closely confining a puppy to his bed strongly inhibits urination and defecation. This means the pup will need to relieve himself when released from the crate each hour. You will then be there to show the puppy the right spot, reward him for eliminating in the right spot, and then enjoy a short play/training session with the delightfully empty puppy.

Introducing the crate

Before confining your puppy to his crate (doggie den), you first need to teach him to love the crate and to love confinement.

This is so easy to do. Stuff a couple of hollow chewtoys with kibble and the occasional treat. Let your puppy sniff the stuffed chewtoys and then place them in the crate and shut the door with your puppy on the outside. Usually it takes just a few seconds for your puppy to beg you to open the door and let him inside. In no time at all, your pup will be happily preoccupied with his chewtoys.

When leaving the puppy in his long-stay confinement area, tie the stuffed chewtoys to the inside of the crate and leave the crate door open. Thus, the puppy can choose whether he wants to explore the small area or lie down on his bed in his crate and try to extricate the kibble and treats from his chewtoys.

Basically, the stuffed chewtoys are confined to the crate and the puppy is given the option of coming or going at will. Most puppies choose to rest comfortably inside the crate with stuffed chewtoys for entertainment. This technique works especially well if your puppy is not fed kibble from a bowl but only from chewtoys or by hand, as lures and rewards in

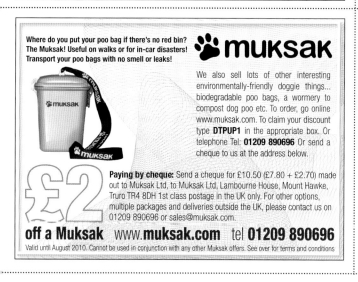

TERMS AND CONDITIONS:

1. Voucher can only be redeemed once in a single transaction per household. **2.** Offer cannot be used in conjunction with any other offer from this company. **3.** Offer strictly non-transferable. **4.** Voucher value 0.001p.

This voucher entitles you to £5 off any variety of Burns Real Food (min 7.5kg). For your nearest stockist call 0800 018 18 90 or check online at www.burnspet.co.uk. Offer ends 30th November 2010.

Please tick your requirement

7.5kg ☐   15kg ☐

If you do not wish to be contacted by Burns Pet Nutrition or its partners, please tick here ☐

Stockists - This voucher must be returned to Burns by 31 December 2010 and can only be credited if all the details have been completed and conditions met. The voucher may only be used once against a purchase of Burns and is non-transferable. Only one voucher per purchase. Voucher value 0.001p. Burns reserves the right to refuse payment of any mis-redeemed vouchers.

Burns Pet Nutrition Ltd, Freepost SWC 4429, Kidwelly SA17 5ZY.

Customer details

Name ....
Address ....
....
....
Postcode ....
Email ....

Stockist details

Name ....
Address ....
....
....
Postcode ....
Email ....

ADPERPUP1210

Petplan
the pet people

Activate your FREE cover right now!

Here are 4 reasons why:

- **4 weeks free cover*** from the moment you activate, with no obligation including £2,000 vet fees cover
- **We're the UK's No.1 pet insurance provider.** (Datamonitor - August 2008)
- **1 in 3 pets may require urgent veterinary treatment this year** (Petplan)

This voucher can not be used in conjunction with any other offer. Telephone calls may be monitored and recorded. Petplan is a trading name of Allianz Insurance plc which is authorised and regulated by the Financial Services Authority (FSA). Registered office: 57 Ladymead, Guildford, Surrey GU1 1DB. *Terms, conditions and excesses apply. Immediate cover for injury, cover for illness starts after 14 days.

the pet people

To activate your free cover call **0800 107 1164** Quote MAG4WKS
or visit **petplan.co.uk**

TERMS AND CONDITIONS:

1. Voucher can only be redeemed once in a single transaction per household. **2.** Offer cannot be used in conjunction with any other offer from this company. **3.** Offer strictly non-transferable. **4.** Voucher value 0.001p.

TERMS AND CONDITIONS:

1. Voucher can only be redeemed once in a single transaction per household. **2.** Offer cannot be used in conjunction with any other offer from this company. **3.** Offer strictly non-transferable. **4.** Voucher value 0.001p.

TERMS AND CONDITIONS:

1. Voucher can only be redeemed once in a single transaction per household. **2.** Offer cannot be used in conjunction with any other offer from this company. **3.** Offer strictly non-transferable. **4.** Voucher value 0.001p.

ORDER FORM

To order by credit or debit card, or if having trouble deciding the ideal size for your pup, telephone **01276 858880** during office hours, or post the order to: Housetraining Offer, The Dog House, 4 Bonseys Lane, Chobham, Surrey, GU24 8JJ. If unsure about the size of crate, please tell us the breed of pup **enquiries@dogstodaymagazine.co.uk**

You can photocopy this offer or copy out the details if you prefer.

Orders will be despatched by carrier ASAP. (No deliveries on weekends or bank holidays.)

CRATES

Small	£25.00	☐
Medium	£35.00	☐
Large	£45.00	☐
Extra-large	£55.00	☐
Huge	£60.00	☐

PENS

Puppy play pen	£89.99	☐
High-sided pen	£99.99	☐

Plus carriage UK mainland £7.50, £3 second item.
Highlands and Islands, offshore including Channel Islands £15 per item.

Total enclosed: £ ☐

NAME

ADDRESS

POSTCODE

DAYTIME TELEPHONE NUMBER (IN CASE OF QUERY)

I enclose a cheque payable to Pet Subjects Ltd ☐

Please debit my Visa ☐ Mastercard ☐ Maestro ☐ Delta ☐ Amex ☐

Card Number

Expiry Date   /   Valid from   /   Security No
(last three digits on strip of back of card)

Card issue no (Maestro only)

Signature   Date:

Puppy models...
It could be yours!

Would you like your puppy to be featured on the pages of *Dogs Today* magazine - or even on the front cover? Would you enjoy a complimentary photoshoot with Tim Rose, one of the best dog photographers in the world?

Our photoshoots are relaxed affairs, taking place in Slough on a weekday. Some pups may be flash-phobic and not enjoy the experience, but most young dogs will love their 15 minutes of fame, especially as we use reward-based methods and tasty chicken and bacon treats to encourage puppies to pose. If your puppy has not yet mastered how to sit and stay, modern technology means that we can remove hands and much more - so we remain undefeated by even the most testing subject!

How? It's simple - just email Chloe@dogstodaymagazine. co.uk with a photo of your new best friend, some contact details, and why you think your puppy should be featured in the magazine. Or you can post your puppy's details to Chloé Addo, Model Dogs, *Dogs Today*, The Dog House, 4 Bonseys Lane, Chobham, Surrey GU24 8JJ.

Don't be shy; contact us today! Let us capture the cuteness of your new puppy!

training. To use this method, each morning measure out the puppy's daily ration of food into a bag to avoid overfeeding.

What to do at bed-time
You choose where your pup sleeps at night. If you want your pup in his long-term confinement area overnight, or in a dog crate in the kitchen, or your bedroom, that's fine. Or if you want the pup tethered in his bed beside your bed, that's fine too. What is important, though, is that the puppy is confined to a small area

and settles down quickly and quietly. Offer the puppy an intelligently stuffed chew-toy and he will likely chew himself to sleep in no time at all.

Once you have housetrained and chew-trained your puppy and he has learned to settle down quickly and quietly, you may allow your pup to choose where he would like to sleep - indoors, outdoors, upstairs, downstairs, in your bedroom, or in your bed - just as long as his choice is fine with you.

It is a good idea to practise

the night-time routine during the day when you are awake and in good humour. Don't wait to train your puppy until you are tired and ready for bed and your grouchy brain is barely functioning. During the day, practise having your puppy settle down in his bed or crate, both in the same room as you and in different rooms so that he gets used to sleeping alone.

Should your pup whine at night-time, check on him every five minutes. Talk softly to him and stroke him gently for a minute, and then go back to bed. But do not overdo it. The idea is to reassure your puppy, not to train him to whine for late-night attention. Also, do not go straight to sleep, for you'll probably be checking on your puppy after 10 minutes. Once the puppy eventually falls asleep, I find it enjoyable to check on him and stroke him for four or five minutes. A lot of people dare not do this for fear they will wake the little critter, but it has always worked well for me.

If you follow the above routine, you'll find it will take less than seven nights before your puppy learns to go to sleep quickly and quietly.

The doggie toilet

For the best doggie toilet, equip a litter box or cover a piece of old linoleum with what will be the dog's eventual toilet material. For example, for rural and suburban pups who will eventually be taught to relieve themselves outside on earth or grass, lay down a roll of turf. For urban puppies who will eventually be taught to eliminate at the curbside, lay down a couple of thin concrete tiles. Your puppy will soon develop a very strong natural preference for eliminating on similar outdoor surfaces whenever he can.

If you have a dog toilet area in your back garden, in addition to the indoor playroom toilet, take your pup to his outdoor toilet in the yard whenever you release him from his doggie den.

Training your dog to use an outdoor toilet

For the first few weeks, take your puppy outside on the leash. Hurry to his toilet area and then stand still to allow the puppy to circle (as he would normally do before eliminating).

Reward your puppy each time he 'goes' in the designated spot. If you have a fenced garden, you may later take your puppy outside off-leash and let him choose where he would like to eliminate. But make sure you reward him differentially according to how close he hits ground zero. Offer one treat for doing it outside quickly, two treats for doing it within, say, five yards of the doggie toilet, three treats for within two yards, and five treats for a bullseye. ▶

Should your pup whine at night-time, check on him every five minutes. Talk softly to him and stroke him gently for a minute, and then go back to bed. But do not overdo it. The idea is to reassure your puppy, not to train him to whine for late-night attention

There are many types of stuffable chewtoys available these days, but the Kong is a must-have for all dog owners. They are virtually indestructible, bounce unpredictably to keep your dog engaged, and can keep them occupied for hours if stuffed correctly...

- Be inventive when stuffing - there are thousands of different recipe combinations! The key is to get a good balance. If the contents are too easy to dislodge, your dog will finish the Kong in minutes. On the other hand, if the contents are too difficult to get out, your dog will eventually lose interest. So use a mixture of hard and soft stuffings.

- Put something really tasty and smelly in the bottom of the Kong - dried liver works a treat or, if you can stand the pong, some dried tripe pieces. These will keep the Kong super-appealing to your dog until the very end! Then, in the middle section, put some dried kibble, and then squish in some cheese or peanut butter to keep everything inside. In the top part, pop some things that can be easily chewed and licked out, to get your dog started - maybe some Kong Stuffer paté (from pet shops) with some dried kibble, or some cream cheese.

- If your dog empties it quickly, get tougher next time!

- Have fun experimenting. Perhaps melt some cheese and let it cool and harden, to make it more difficult to extract from the Kong, or you can even freeze a Kong and make some Kong lollies for outdoor use in the summer.

- And remember, as your pup grows, so should the Kong! Make sure you get the correct size for his jaws.

Housetraining FAQs...

Why release the pup every hour?

Puppies have a 45-minute bladder capacity at three weeks of age, 75-minute capacity at eight weeks, 90-minute capacity at 12 weeks and two-hour capacity at 18 weeks. Releasing your puppy every hour offers you an hourly opportunity to reward your dog for using a designated toilet area. You do not have to do this precisely each hour, but it is much easier to remember to do so each hour on the hour.

Why run the puppy to the toilet?

If you take your time getting your puppy to his doggie toilet, you may find that he pees or poops en route. Hurrying your puppy tends to jiggle his bowels and bladder so that he really wants to go the moment you let him stand still and sniff his toilet area.

Why not just put the puppy outside?

Of course you can. But the whole point of predicting when your puppy wants to relieve himself is so you can show him where and offer well-deserved praise and reward. Thus your puppy will learn where you would like him to go. Also, if you see your puppy eliminate, you know that he is

empty; you may then allow your empty puppy supervised exploration of the house for a while before returning him to his den.

Why instruct the pup to eliminate?

By instructing and rewarding him for eliminating, you will teach your pup to go on command. Eliminating on cue is a boon when you are travelling with your dog and in other time-constrained situations. Ask your pup to "Hurry up," "Do your business," "Go pee and poop," or use some other socially acceptable, euphemistic eliminatory command.

Why give the puppy three minutes?

Usually, a young pup will urinate within 30 seconds of being released from short-term confinement, but it may take one or two minutes for him to defecate. It is certainly worthwhile to allow your pup three minutes to complete his business.

What if the puppy doesn't go?

Your puppy will be more likely to eliminate if you stand still and let him circle around you on-leash. If your puppy does not eliminate within the allotted time, no biggie! Simply pop the

pup back in his crate and try again in half an hour. Repeat the process over and over until he does eliminate. Eventually, your puppy will eliminate outdoors and you will be able to reward him. Therefore, on subsequent hourly trips to his toilet your puppy will be likely to eliminate promptly.

Why praise the puppy?

It is far better to express your emotions when praising your puppy for getting it right, than when reprimanding the poor pup for getting it wrong. So really praise that pup: "Gooooooooood puppy!" Housetraining is no time for understated thank yous. Don't be embarrassed about praising your puppy. Embarrassed dog owners usually end up with housesoiling problems. Really reward your puppy. Tell your puppy that he has done a most wonderful and glorious thing!

Why offer treats?

Many owners - especially men - seem incapable of convincingly praising their puppies. Consequently, it might be a good idea to give the pup a food treat or two (or three) for his effort. Input for output! "Wow! My owner's great. Every time I pee or poop outside, she gives me a treat. I never get yummy treats when I do it on the couch. I can't wait for my owner to come home so I can go out in the garden and cash in my urine and faeces for food treats!" In fact, why not keep some treats in a screw-top jar handy to the doggie toilet?

Why freeze-dried liver?

Housetraining is one of those times when you want to pull out all of the stops. Take my word for it: when it comes to housetraining, use the Ferrari of dog treats - freeze-dried liver.

What should I do if I've done all the above and I catch the puppy in the act of making a mistake?

Pick up a rolled newspaper and give yourself a smack! Obviously you did not follow the instructions. Who allowed the urine-and-faeces-filled puppy to have free-range access to your house? You!

Should you ever reprimand or punish your puppy when you catch him in the act, all he will learn is to eliminate in secret - that is, never again in your untrustworthy presence. Thus you will have created an owner-absent housesoiling problem.

If you ever catch your pup in the act of making a mistake that was your fault, at the very most you can quickly, softly, but urgently implore your pup, "Outside, outside, outside!" The tone and urgency of your voice communicates that you want your puppy to do something promptly, and the meaning of the words instruct the puppy where. Your response will have limited effect on the present mistake, but it helps prevent future mistakes.

Never reprimand your dog in a manner that is not instructive. Non-specific reprimands only create more problems (owner-absent misbehaviour) as well as

Reward your puppy each time he 'goes' in the designated spot. But make sure you reward him differentially according to how close he hits ground zero. Offer one treat for doing it outside quickly, two treats for doing it within, say, five yards of the doggie toilet, three treats for within two yards, and five treats for a bullseye

frightening the pup and eroding the puppy-owner relationship. Your puppy is not a bad puppy. On the contrary, your puppy is a good puppy that has been forced to misbehave because his owner could not, or would not, follow simple instructions.

Home alone

When you are at home, it is also a good idea to occasionally confine your puppy to his puppy playroom (long-term confinement area) as a practice-run for your absence. Occasional long-term confinement when you are at home allows you to monitor your pup's behaviour so you have some idea how he will act when you are gone.

If your puppy barks or whines when confined to his short- or long-term confinement area, reward-train him to rest quietly.

Sit next to your puppy's crate or just outside his puppy playroom and busy yourself by reading a book, working on the computer, or watching television. Completely ignore your puppy while he vocalises, but each time he stops barking, immediately praise him calmly and offer a piece of kibble.

After half a dozen repetitions, progressively increase the shushtime required for each successive piece of kibble - two seconds, three seconds, five, eight, 15, 20, etc. Thereafter, periodically praise and reward your puppy every few minutes or so if he remains resting quietly.

If barking is still a problem after a couple of weeks, read my *Barking* booklet or *Doctor Dunbar's Good Little Dog Book* to learn how to teach your puppy to 'woof and shush' on cue. •

If you're using the methods outlined here, yet still having problems with housesoiling or house destruction after one week, read Dr Ian Dunbar's *Housetraining and Chewing Behaviour* booklets. See www.dogstardaily.com for more information

Still having problems?

A good training class will help you to learn positive training techniques so you can teach your puppy good manners and voice cues easily and quickly. It will also help you overcome any minor behaviour problems and give your puppy a happy, well-balanced start in life. **Gwen Bailey** shows you what to look out for when choosing a puppy class...

Royalty-free stock image

Positive Training

✓ Training methods should be kind and effective. Choose a class where owners are encouraged to use food and toys to reward actions they want.

✓ Make sure the trainer is rewarding the correct action immediately and is demonstrating techniques that make a noticeable difference to the puppy's actions.

✓ Avoid any trainer that uses aversive methods, such as a lead jerk, water spray, shouting or worse, to achieve their goals.

✓ Puppies and owners learn much faster and more happily if only positive techniques are taught and practised.

Training classes vary in standard and it is important to find a good one. There are still a lot of trainers in the UK who insist on using outdated, punishment-based ideas, on both puppies and humans! To avoid finding yourself in such a class, you will need to do some research to locate a good one.

The worst thing to do is call a number from the first advert you see, sign up and hope for the best. Instead, ask everyone you know and all dog professionals around you for their recommendations. Try local vets, dog wardens, rescue homes, groomers and pet shops. Contact the trainers and, once you have a short-list, go along to your favourite to watch, without your puppy at first, to find out what happens there. If you like what you see, book quickly to be sure of a place on their next course.

Make an assessment based on the following criteria:

● Positive training methods for training puppies and humans, using praise, food treats and games with toys

● Training is effective for both people and puppies so that all are learning and progressing

● Calm, ordered class

● Any off-lead play is carefully managed and supervised with just a few puppies off-lead for short periods of time

● Play is carefully managed to protect shy pups and cool down rough players

● People and puppies are having fun

It's easy to feel overwhelmed with all the feeding choices that face new puppy owners, but simplicity is key says **John Burns...**

For a number of years I recommended that my veterinary practice clients avoid feeding commercial pet foods but instead fed a home-made diet of brown rice, vegetables and chicken, fish or meat sold for human consumption. Although a number of people were able to follow this recommendation, and achieved remarkable improvements in the health of their pets, many found that preparing food for their dog at home was simply too daunting a task.

Now that I have a dog of my own, I realise what a burden this is and I doubt if I would be able to do it myself. I am sure I lost many clients in this way.

I eventually decided that to manage health through diet, the food would have to be convenient and readily available.

Burns Real Food is based on the home-made diet that I used to recommend. There are no secret or magic ingredients; there are no added pharmacologically active supplements or ingredients. As the name implies, Burns Real Food is just that: a simple food that is intended to allow the body to function as it should.

Being taken away from your mother and siblings into a strange environment can be daunting, so I recommend only offering your new puppy a very small amount of food at his first feeding time. Feeding when stressed can lead to digestive upset. Obviously, you must provide fresh drinking water at all times and provide toys and entertainment for your puppy.

Do not fill the puppy with treats and sweets on top of his daily allowance. Instead take whatever treats are given out of the daily allowance. Your puppy's diet will then not exceed his needs, as this could cause health problems and weight gain.

Pet owners are naturally anxious to ensure that the growing puppy receives adequate levels of nutrients to sustain growth and development. Breeders and owners love to see plump, roly-poly puppies, which seem to epitomise good health and proper care. Fat babies were once admired in the same way, but this is now frowned on by health professionals.

In practice, more health problems result from over-feeding than from lack of adequate nutrition. Although severe under-feeding will stunt growth, slight under-feeding during growth will actually reduce health problems in adulthood.

There is undisputed evidence that a high intake of protein and fat during puppyhood leads to skeletal disorders, such as hip dysplasia, obesity and a shortened lifespan. Behavioural problems, especially hyperactivity, can often be attributed to the same cause. Skin diseases, which used to be seen mainly in older dogs, now seem to be prevalent in young dogs as well.

In spite of this evidence, most commercial pet foods for puppies have very high levels of protein and fat, and this is even promoted as a virtue. The key to having a healthy puppy is to feed enough protein to ensure a slow rate of growth rather than for the puppy to shoot up quickly. A puppy who grows slowly will still realise his full growth potential but may take a little longer to reach full size.

The needs of puppies vary tremendously, so recommended feeding amounts should be treated with suspicion. Good judgement and experience are better guides. If in doubt, consult a nutritionist.

Burns Mini Bites have been developed to ensure that puppies' requirements are met but not exceeded. The levels of protein and fat are only slightly higher than for adult food. Like other Burns foods, Mini Bites are made with ingredients that are highly digestible so that the puppy will be able to utilise the food rather than pass much of it as faeces. As with other Burns foods, Mini Bites will minimise the amount of harmful waste matter within the system.

Although many health problems or weaknesses have a hereditary basis, correct diet can minimise the effects. Weakness of the digestive system, as in the German Shepherd, or a tendency to develop eczema, as in the West Highland Terrier, can be avoided by correct diet. Hip dysplasia has been shown to be aggravated by incorrect diet during growth and it is likely that other developmental disorders of the skeleton are also diet-related.

Some health-care professionals recommend that puppies should not be exercised, as they believe that it will damage the developing bones and joints. This makes as little sense as recommending that children should not have exercise until adulthood! Exercise promotes good muscle tone and well-developed bones and joints, as well as providing social interaction. As mentioned above, developmental defects of the skeleton are caused not by exercise but by poor diet.

Enjoy your puppy; the food choices you make at this age can shape his entire life. I hope the voucher at the back of this book will come in handy.

www.burnspet.co.uk

MINI BITES
A complete food for all puppies and toy breed adult dogs

15 KG

Roly-poly puppy?

Studies show that plump puppies are more likely to develop joint conditions as adult dogs.

Burns Mini Bites were developed to contain controlled levels of protein and fat. This promotes a slow, steady growth rate resulting in a leaner, healthier puppy. Call our team of expert nutritionists to help you find the right diet for your pet.

Affenpinscher

Character sketch

This is a comical animal who loves to amuse his owners. He's a hardy, easy dog, with no real vices.

The Affenpinscher is bright and knowledgeable. Although he is small and doesn't need a colossal amount of exercise, he does need mental stimulation. Play at home and in the garden is also important and will develop his incredible mind.

The Affenpinscher likes contact and communication: the more an owner can talk to him, the better. Be careful when introducing other pets, as the breed can be jealous and possessive - although ultimately they could become the best of friends.

As a companion, the Affenpinscher is a pure delight and full of fun. It really is a case of 'to know him is to love him'.

Special considerations

Do not overfeed the adult, as he tends to get fat. Give him plenty of things to stimulate his busy mind.

History

Originally kept on German farms as working dogs with the task of keeping down vermin. The Affen's ancestors were probably bigger, but it's likely that a smaller dog was bred to catch mice in household kitchens. By the late 18th century, Affenpinschers were being kept purely as companions in Germany and elsewhere. They also performed in circuses and cabaret during the 1920s and 30s. Like many European breeds, their fortunes took a perilous turn during the Second World War and they came close to extinction. Their numbers have never really recovered in their native Germany and it's thought that there are currently more Affenpinschers in the US than the rest of the world put together.

Like this?
Check out these alternatives:

- Chihuahua
- Miniature Schnauzer
- Miniature Pinscher
- Norfolk Terrier
- Scottish Terrier

Vital statistics

Height:	24-28 cms
Weight:	3-4 kgs
Exercise:	●○○○
Grooming:	●○○○
Noise:	●●○○
Food bill:	£6 per week on average

Country of origin:	Germany
Original function:	Vermin control and watchdog
Availability:	Difficult

Colours:	Solid black; grey shading permitted
Coat type:	Rough and harsh; short and dense on some parts, shaggy on others
Coat care:	Twice-weekly brushing with a firm brush and comb

Health

Average life span:	13 years
Hereditary disorders:	Patella luxation
Hip dysplasia:	16 (breed mean score)

Suitability

Exercise:	A daily walk and some play in the garden
Ease of training:	Early, patient training needed, as this is a very determined dog
Temperament with children:	Good, but all children should be taught to respect him
With dogs?	Okay
With cats?	Good, but introduce carefully
Town or country dog?	Either
Would he happily live in a flat or apartment?	Yes, with adequate attention from the owner
Natural guard dog?	No, too small - but he makes a good watchdog
Attitude to strangers?	Wary

Want to know more?

Breed advice: Val Kemeny 01895 462988; Mrs C K Mumby 01472 507091
Breed rescue: Mrs A Teasdale 01932 847679; Linda McGill 0115 933 2263

Like this?
Check out these
alternatives:

- Borzoi
- Deerhound
- Greyhound
- Whippet

Special considerations
The Afghan needs careful, patient and kind training, or there will be resentment. He dislikes being alone.

Character sketch

The Afghan Hound pretends to be elegant and haughty, but in reality he is playful - even clownish. They are extremely playful as pups, and remain young at heart with their family throughout adulthood. Like all hounds, he may become stone-deaf when his hunting blood is stirred, so early recall training is essential. He has a reputation as a 'dumb blonde', but training is possible with the right motivation - and a lot of patience! Properly reared in the right environment, the Afghan is an affectionate pet, devoted to his family, and he will be a talking point wherever he goes.

History

Part of the breed's mystery stems from the fact that Afghanistan has been inaccessible to outsiders for much of history. The Afghan Hound was unknown to the Western world until the 19th century and anything before that is largely guesswork. Something resembling the Afghan Hound has been around for a very long time. Researchers at the Canine Studies Institute in Ohio recently traced the Afghan back 6,000 years to the Middle East region.

The Afghan's ancestors were trained for a wide variety of tasks appropriate to where they lived, including hunting deer, jackals, gazelles, wolves and snow leopards, and working alongside trained falcons. They were also used as guard dogs and as herders of sheep and goats.

Afghan Hounds were first brought into the UK in the 1890s by British officers returning from a tour of duty on what was then the Indian-Afghanistan border.

Vital statistics

Height:	63-74 cms
Weight:	Around 29.5 kgs
Exercise:	●●●●
Grooming:	●●●●
Noise:	●●○○
Food bill:	£9 per week on average

Country of origin:	Afghanistan
Original function:	Hunting
Availability:	Difficult

Colours:	All colours acceptable
Coat type:	Long and silky
Coat care:	Should be groomed at least every other day

Health

Average life span:	11½ years
Hereditary disorders:	No problems known to breeders
Hip dysplasia:	8 (breed mean score)

Suitability

Exercise:	As much as you can give - then more!
Ease of training:	Patience needed! Some more trainable than others
Temperament with children:	Good with respectful kids
With dogs?	Good
With cats?	Okay with his 'own' family cats, if socialised early
Town or country dog?	Prefers country
Would he happily live in a flat or apartment?	Yes, with adequate exercise
Natural guard dog?	Will protect his owner and property
Attitude to strangers?	Aloof

Want to know more?

 Breed advice & rescue: Mrs J Chilton 0161 428 4789

History

The Akita is an ancient breed, with its ancestors dating back 4,000 years. The Japanese believe it to be of Chinese origin developed from a superb hunting dog known as a Montagi Nu from about the 7th century. This breed was a renowned hunter of black bears. Because of its toughness, and indifference to cold, it became a prized all-purpose hunting breed. The fifth shogun, General Tsunayoshi, (around 1700 AD) was a devotee of the breed and built a massive palace solely for his dogs. One of the first laws he passed was that anyone who injured or killed an Akita would be subject to imprisonment or even death.

This spoilt life was not to last long. By the mid 1800s, dog fighting became the mode and the Akita was bred to the Tosa Inu, to make for a tougher animal. Dog fighting was banned early in the 20th century, and the breed became better known in Japan, with its handsome looks and loyalty winning it the title of 'National Treasure' in 1934.

Like this?
Check out these alternatives:

- Alaskan Malamute
- German Shepherd Dog
- Japanese Shiba Inu
- Tibetan Mastiff
- Samoyed

Special considerations

They must be trained from an early age with great patience in short periods. Will get bored easily.

Character sketch

Because of the Akita's tendency to dominate, he must be thoroughly socialised as a young puppy and trained firmly with kindness and patience. Properly raised, the Akita makes a loyal and protective dog suitable for an active country family who makes the effort to understand the breed. The Akita is very self-assured but tends to show dominance towards other dogs. This breed is very loyal and affectionate to his own family.

Vital statistics

Height:	61-71 cms
Weight:	Approximately 40-54 kgs
Exercise:	●●●○
Grooming:	●●●○
Noise:	●○○○
Food bill:	£10 per week on average

Country of origin:	Japan
Original function:	Hunting and guarding
Availability:	Moderate
Colours:	Any colour, including white, brindle and pinto with or without a mask
Coat type:	Harsh stand-off outer coat; dense and soft undercoat
Coat care:	Weekly brush and comb, more when moulting

Health

Average life span:	11 years
Hereditary disorders:	Parents should be eye-tested and tested for sebaceous adenitis (a skin disease)
Hip dysplasia:	11 (breed mean score)

Suitability

Exercise:	From moderate to lots!
Ease of training:	Easy to housetrain; obedience training can be difficult
Temperament with children:	Dependent on treatment by children; needs to be supervised
With dogs?	Not good
With cats?	Okay with his 'own'; may hunt others
Town or country dog?	Country
Would he happily live in a flat or apartment	Not advisable
Natural guard dog?	Yes
Attitude to strangers?	Suspicious

Want to know more?

Breed advice: Margaret Aylward 020 8924 5478; K Hay 01375 891488
Breed rescue: Japanese Akita Welfare Trust 05062 955217

History

The Alaskan Malamute's origins go so far back in time they are completely obscured. They belong to the Nordic Spitz group and it is believed that their contact with humans stretches back 2,000 years, when they accompanied the migrating tribes from Asia across the Bering Straits to the vast wilderness of Alaska. When settlers arrived in Alaska in the late 1800s they immediately recognised the potential of this big, powerful snow dog and the breed became the main power used to move goods and provisions vast distances.

Special considerations

The Alaskan Malamute has the most wonderful coat, as befits a polar dog, but it requires maximum maintenance. Neglected it becomes a thick matt, a natural breeding ground for fleas. An owner must be prepared for hard work as it needs deep combing three or four times a week with more attention when he moults.

Character sketch

A big, powerful dog, needing a firm, but kind hand. Contented Malamutes are ones that work! The Malamute is very stubborn and males tend toward dominance. They have to be patiently trained from young – shouting and getting angry is counter-productive as the dog will realise his owner is weak and will take advantage. He needs space and plenty of exercise for both his physical and mental well-being. It would be a very good idea for his family to join a club specialising in Husky-type dogs, giving the dog a chance to pull sleds, a trait that is bred into them. In the right hands this dog will enhance any family, his handsome looks with unique facial markings will be a talking point wherever he is and his happy, affectionate nature will endear him to all.

Like this?
Check out these alternatives:

- Akita
- Elkhound
- Japanese Shiba Inu
- Samoyed
- Siberian Husky

Vital statistics

Height:	66-71 cms
Weight:	Around 56 kgs
Exercise:	●●●○
Grooming:	●●○○
Noise:	●●○○
Food bill:	£14 per week on average

Country of origin:	Alaska
Original function:	Sled haulage
Availability:	Moderate

Colours:	Red/white, black/white, grey/white, wolf sable and solid white
Coat type:	Plush – coarse guard coat with thick undercoat
Coat care:	Deep combing three or four times a week - more when moulting

Health

Average life span:	14 years
Hereditary disorders:	Parents should be eye-tested and have had a clear DNA test for hypothyroidism
Hip dysplasia:	13 (breed mean score)

Suitability

Exercise:	Four miles a day is the minimum – it is not possible to wear this dog out!
Ease of training:	Moderate
Temperament with children:	Excellent
With dogs?	Dominant with own breed
With cats?	Okay with own, watch it with others
Town or country dog?	Either
Would he happily live in a flat or apartment?	No
Natural guard dog?	No
Attitude to strangers?	Friendly

Want to know more?

Breed advice: Barbara Stanier 01842 878202
Breed rescue: Julie Cox 01793 613400

American Cocker Spaniel

 ## History

There have been spaniel-type dogs since at least the 14th century. Originally from Spain, these dogs soon became well-known in royal courts across Europe and were prized as hunting companions, while the smaller ones were favoured as ideal companions for ladies.

The terms 'springer' and 'cocker' were first used around 1790, although it wasn't until 1892 that they were officially recognised as two separate breeds by the Kennel Club.

Cocker Spaniels were exported to America in the latter part of the 19th century and were used to hunt woodcock, grouse and pheasant - as they had been in their native country. Over time, the Cocker Spaniels that were living in America went off in a different direction to the ones that had stayed at home. Americans began breeding a slightly smaller, more glamorous dog: the head became rounder, the muzzle shorter and the coat longer, producing a quite different dog to the original Cocker Spaniel.

Like this?
Check out these alternatives:

- Cavalier King Charles Spaniel
- Cocker Spaniel
- King Charles Spaniel
- English Springer Spaniel
- Welsh Springer Spaniel

 ## Character sketch

This happy-go-lucky, ever-wagging dog is playful into old age. 'Merry' is a word often associated with the breed, and they are also keen to work and use their brains. Training, therefore, usually presents few problems, provided the dog is well motivated (most will do anything for food or a toy). They are inquisitive dogs, with a real zest for life, and will want to be at the heart of the action with their family.

Special considerations
Never allow this dog to get fat - he's very greedy and a skilled thief, so be on your guard! Pet dogs are generally kept in a shorter coat.

Vital statistics

Height:	34-39 cms
Weight:	11 kgs
Exercise:	●●●○
Grooming:	●●●●
Noise:	●●○○
Food bill:	£6 per week on average

Country of origin:	Britain, developed in America
Original function:	Working in difficult cover
Availability:	Fairly easy
Colours:	Black, black and tan, brown, buffs (from the deepest red to the palest cream), sable, particolours (black/white, red/white, lemon/white) and tricolours
Coat type:	Very long and silky; flat or slightly wavy
Coat care:	A daily brush and a weekly bath

Health

Average life span:	12 years
Hereditary disorders:	Parents and pups should be eye-tested. DNA test available for metabolic disorder
Hip dysplasia:	Insufficient numbers have been tested

Suitability

Exercise:	Adults require at least two half-hour romps a day, but will happily take more!
Ease of training:	Pretty straightforward
Temperament with children:	Very good, if the children are taught to be respectful
With dogs?	No problems
With cats?	Usually okay, if socialised as puppies
Town or country dog?	Either
Would he happily live in a flat or apartment?	Not ideal
Natural guard dog?	Noisy if intruders are suspected or if the doorbell rings
Attitude to strangers?	Outgoing

Want to know more?

 Breed advice: Karen Caunce 01782 312930
Breed rescue: Mrs Morris 01914 556644

Anatolian Shepherd Dog

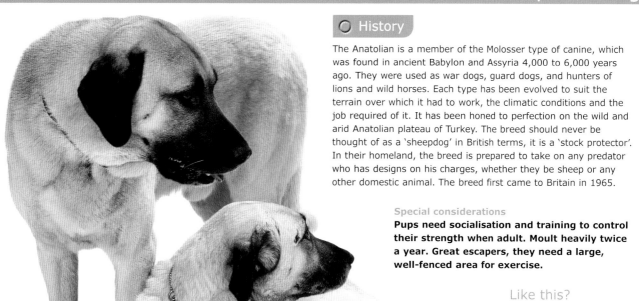

History

The Anatolian is a member of the Molosser type of canine, which was found in ancient Babylon and Assyria 4,000 to 6,000 years ago. They were used as war dogs, guard dogs, and hunters of lions and wild horses. Each type has been evolved to suit the terrain over which it had to work, the climatic conditions and the job required of it. It has been honed to perfection on the wild and arid Anatolian plateau of Turkey. The breed should never be thought of as a 'sheepdog' in British terms, it is a 'stock protector'. In their homeland, the breed is prepared to take on any predator who has designs on his charges, whether they be sheep or any other domestic animal. The breed first came to Britain in 1965.

Special considerations

Pups need socialisation and training to control their strength when adult. Moult heavily twice a year. Great escapers, they need a large, well-fenced area for exercise.

Like this?
Check out these alternatives:

- Great Dane
- Leonberger
- Pyrenean Mountain Dog
- St Bernard
- Tibetan Mastiff

Character sketch

With their working instincts, this is not a breed for everyone - these dogs need things to do. They would be ideal on a farm where they can patrol the fields, protecting everything from chickens to cows. They do not befriend people easily, but, once they understand a person is not a threat, they will become gentle and affectionate.

They are not overly aggressive towards other dogs, but the males are often dominant and don't live well together. Reward-based training from young will pay dividends.

Vital statistics

Height:	71-81 cms
Weight:	41-64 kgs
Exercise:	●●○○
Grooming:	●●●○
Noise:	●○○○
Food bill:	£14 per week on average

Country of origin:	Turkey
Original function:	Livestock protection
Availability:	Difficult

Colours:	All colours; preference for solid cream to fawn with black mask
Coat type:	Short with dense undercoat
Coat care:	Weekly combing and brushing with a firm comb

Health

Average life span:	11 years
Hereditary disorders:	No problems known to breeders
Hip dysplasia:	14 (breed mean score)

Suitability

Exercise:	As much as possible when adult
Ease of training:	Okay with kind, patient training that is started when young
Temperament with children:	Good, but can be clumsy, so not ideal for a family with little ones.
With dogs?	Be careful, males can be dominant
With cats?	Can be okay with his own, if trained and socialised from early puppyhood; likely to hunt others
Town or country dog?	Country
Would he happily live in a flat or apartment?	No
Natural guard dog?	Yes
Attitude to strangers?	Suspicious

Want to know more?

Breed advice: Pat Broadhead 01978 756595
Breed rescue: Roz Carr 01946 822772

History

The Australian outback is no place for a wimpish dog - the climate is harsh and the cattle wild and self-willed. Stockmen in the early 1800s were basically British farm workers and shepherds who found that their collies (who'd travelled with them to Australia) were not hardy enough. Consequently, they set about creating a breed capable of performing demanding work with the minimum of trouble. Dingoes were crossed with imported blue-mottled Northumberland sheepdogs from near the Scottish border. Later crosses may have included descendants of Timmins Biters (Smithfield Collie/dingo crosses), Bull Terriers and Dalmatians. As the result of the infusion of many canine bloods, the breed evolved into a super-energetic, highly intelligent dog, able to work under his own initiative in high temperatures or heavy rainfall.

Character sketch

This family-orientated dog loves to be involved. He has a wicked sense of humour, and, properly trained and socialised, makes an exceptional pet. Not an ideal breed for the first-time dog owner, as he is inclined to exploit what he regards as weaknesses in his owners and can be too independent, assertive and dominant. His enormous energy has to be channelled if he is to live happily in a domestic situation. He learns quickly as he is very intelligent, but is very wary of strangers.

Special considerations
Socialisation from early puppyhood is essential. This breed does not like being left alone and needs lots of human interaction, and mental and physical stimulation.

Like this?
Check out these alternatives:

- Australian Shepherd Dog
- Border Collie
- Collie (Rough)
- Swedish Vallhund

Vital statistics

Height:	43-51 cms
Weight:	17-23 kgs
Exercise:	●●●○
Grooming:	●○○○
Noise:	●●●○
Food bill:	£7 per week on average

Country of origin:	Australia
Original function:	Cattle herding
Availability:	Moderate
Colours:	Blue; mottled or speckled blue; black, blue or tan markings. Red speckle, with or without darker red markings on head
Coat type:	Smooth, double-coated, and harsh to the touch, with a dense undercoat
Coat care:	A weekly brush and comb

Health

Average life span:	15 years
Hereditary disorders:	Parents should be eye-tested. Deafness, patella luxation
Hip dysplasia:	11 (breed mean score)

Suitability

Exercise:	As much as he can get
Ease of training:	Easy with short, frequent lessons administered kindly but firmly
Temperament with children:	Very good, assuming the kids and dogs have been properly trained
With dogs?	Usually okay with their own breed, but not enthusiastic about other breeds
With cats?	Be careful - some good, some bad
Town or country dog?	Country
Would he happily live in a flat or apartment?	Yes, with adequate company, exercise and stimulation
Natural guard dog?	Yes
Attitude to strangers?	Quite suspicious

Want to know more?

Breed advice: Pearl Chetwynd 01497 820567
Breed rescue: Stella Smyth 0118 979 3399

Character sketch

Properly reared and trained, the Australian Shepherd Dog is a highly intelligent companion who is utterly devoted to his family. He will guard the territory and should never exhibit a malicious streak. Two types within the breed are emerging: those that are keen and active, and those that are more laidback. With some reservations, Aussies are one of the finest pet dogs a family can have, but the former type is not a dog to own unless you are prepared to train him with patience and kindness and give him a busy life.

Like this?
Check out these alternatives:

- Belgian Shepherd Dog (Tervueren)
- Border Collie
- Collie (Rough)
- Hovawart

Special considerations
The 'Aussie' thrives on human companionship and most need a hobby/sport to occupy them.

History

Despite being named 'Australian', the breed could have come from the Basque country in northern Spain before being popularised and developed in America. Australia was just a stopping-off point in their evolution. The Spanish merino sheep was a great wool producer by the 19th century, and they were exported to Australia and America direct from Spain and other European countries. Their shepherds took with them the dogs they considered most efficient. During their stay in Australia, the Spanish dogs probably mixed with other types of sheepdogs.

It was in the early 1900s, when the sheep industry in the USA began burgeoning, that American livestock-men started to value these highly intelligent working dogs, but it was 50 years before the breed came to the notice of dog fanciers. In 1957 the first Australian Shepherd Dog Club was formed in Arizona. Since then, the breed has blossomed into being a popular show dog and pet.

Vital statistics

Height:	46-58 cms
Weight:	18 27 kgs
Exercise:	●●●●
Grooming:	●●○○
Noise:	●●●○
Food bill:	£7 per week on average

Country of origin:	Spain/USA
Original function:	Working sheep
Availability:	Difficult

Colours:	Black tricolour, red tricolour, red merle, blue merle
Coat type:	Double coat, moderately coarse
Coat care:	Regular brushing

Health

Average life span:	$14^{1}/_{2}$ years
Hereditary disorders:	Parents and pups should be eye-tested DNA test available for Ivermectin sensitivity
Hip dysplasia:	10 (breed mean score)

Suitability

Exercise:	Virtually inexhaustible! A great slimming aid!
Ease of training:	Moderate
Temperament with children:	No problems
With dogs?	Okay
With cats?	Okay with his own, if properly socialised and introduced; be careful with others
Town or country dog?	Country
Would he happily live in a flat or apartment?	No
Natural guard dog?	Yes
Attitude to strangers?	Reserved

Want to know more?

Breed advice: Sharon Gladwell-Hunt 01736 756043; Lydia Brown 01274 619516
Breed rescue: Julie Blackburn 0161 718 9285

History

The Basenji has been a domesticated breed since before 2700BC. There is no doubt that the Egyptians knew the Basenji; when it first appeared in their works of art, it looked much the same as it does today. It seems to have arrived in Egypt already developed, but its actual origins are unclear. Certainly, pariah dogs (semi-wild scavengers) of the Middle East and Asian countries bear a close resemblance to the breed; perhaps traders brought them to the Egyptian coasts.

After the Egyptian empire went into decline, the breed apparently disappeared and it wasn't until the 1860s, when the African pygmy tribes were discovered, that the breed was found again. The pygmies used the Basenji for hunting, and they wore wooden bells (clappers) round their necks, so the hunters knew where they were in the dense undergrowth. They were, and still are, the perfect hunting companion.

Special considerations
These 'heat-seeking missiles' love the warmth, and don't usually like to go out in the rain. The hunting instinct is very strong.

Character sketch

One of the hallmarks of the Basenji is the peculiar sound they make, as their larynxes are slightly different to other breeds. They are not entirely 'barkless' - they can make an odd 'woof', but they don't do it very often.

Although highly intelligent, they are not the easiest breed to train; they have been a hunting breed for millennia and the instinct is ingrained. They are extraordinarily brave and have even been known to defend their owners against leopards.

They are very playful and can live with older children happily, but generally they are too active for younger ones. In the home they are meticulously clean.

Like this?
Check out these alternatives:

- Beagle
- Japanese Shiba Inu

Vital statistics

Height:	40-43 cms
Weight:	9.5-11 kgs
Exercise:	●●●○
Grooming:	●○○○
Noise:	●○○○
Food bill:	£5 per week on average

Country of origin:	Africa
Original function:	Hunting
Availability:	Difficult

Colours:	Black and white, red and white, black, tan and white, brindle; white on feet, chest and tail
Coat type:	Short, sleek and close
Coat care:	Weekly brushing or polishing with a hound glove

Health

Average life span:	15 years
Hereditary disorders:	Parents and pups should be eye-tested. DNA test available for blood disorder
Hip dysplasia:	7 (breed mean score)

Suitability

Exercise:	Adult dogs should be walked for two to three miles a day
Ease of training:	Difficult
Temperament with children:	Not advisable in a home with under-fives
With dogs?	They need watching
With cats?	Not good
Town or country dog?	Country
Would he happily live in a flat or apartment?	Not really
Natural guard dog?	Will warn of the approach of strangers
Attitude to strangers?	Aloof

Want to know more?

 Breed advice: Mrs Constance Graham 01925 756622; Jenny Startup 01462 893714; Kim Ellis 01980 653109
Breed rescue: Rusty Grayson 01457 878747

History

'Bas' means 'low' in French and the earliest record of the word 'Basset' appears in a 1585 book on hunting. Hunting was considered a noble art in medieval France and dogs were bred with great care - a tradition upheld by the friars of St Hubert Abbey, who bred what became known as the St Hubert Hound, which is related to modern-day Bassets and Bloodhounds.

Bassets were first shown in France in 1863. It was around this time that Sir Everett Millais took a shine to the Basset Hound while he was looking at Dachshunds at a dog show in France. He brought a Basset home with him in 1874 and the dog was given its UK show debut the following year. Millais' continued interest in Bassets earned him the title of 'father of the breed'.

Like this?
Check out these alternatives:

- Beagle
- Bloodhound
- Petit Basset Griffon Vendeen

Character sketch

He may look melancholic, but the Basset is a happy-go-lucky dog, full of spirit and humour. A devoted family dog, the Basset gives great affection to all.

He may be low, but the Basset is not small. This is a big dog on short legs. At home he can be a lazy lump, but, once he's stirred to action, he'll run and play with the best of them.

Although he is intelligent, he is not the easiest to train. As with all hunting dogs, the Basset has a stubborn, independent streak, and can be deaf when on a scent, which can occasionally drive an owner mad!

Special considerations
Does not like the wet. Keep him in dry conditions. Males can be stubborn. It is important to keep the ears and wrinkles clean and dry.

Vital statistics

Height:	33-38 cms
Weight:	22.5-34 kgs
Exercise:	●●○○
Grooming:	●●○○
Noise:	●●○○
Food bill:	£7 per week for an adult dog

Country of origin:	France/Britain
Original function:	Hunting
Availability:	Moderate

Colours:	Black, white and tan; any hound colour
Coat type:	Short, close and not too fine
Coat care:	A weekly brush and polish with a hound glove

Health

Average life span:	12 years
Hereditary disorders:	Parents and pups should be eye-tested, elbow dysplasia. DNA test available for immune system disorder
Hip dysplasia:	Insufficient numbers have been tested

Suitability

Exercise:	An enormous amount when adult
Ease of training:	Difficult - requires kind persistence
Temperament with children:	Excellent
With dogs?	Affable
With cats?	Can learn to live happily with cats, but is likely to chase other people's cats
Town or country dog?	Prefers the country
Would he happily live in a flat or apartment?	No
Natural guard dog?	No
Attitude to strangers?	Friendly

Want to know more?

Breed advice: Colin Wells 01964 542744
Breed rescue: Basset Hound Welware 01257 451553

History

The Beagle has been used for hunting for many centuries in Britain. Prince William of Orange had packs of Beagles, as did George IV and Prince Albert. Geoffrey Chaucer's *Canterbury Tales* mentions "small houndes" that were owned by the Prioress.

Elizabeth I kept miniature Beagles, which were reputed to be under 25cm high. They were known as Glove Beagles because they were said to be small enough to fit into a lady's glove.

A book called *The Sportsman's Cabinet,* published in 1803, recommends hunting with packs of Beagles for "gentlemen labouring under infirmity" and even "ladies of the greatest timidity". Beagles have a slower pace and a smaller range than their leggier hound cousins, which is why the remaining packs of Beagles still operating in the UK are foot-hunts.

Character sketch

Beagles are great characters, exhibiting independence and a great love of their family. They are easier to manage than other hunting hounds and in America, they have become the archetypal family pet.

Beagles are a paradox. Outside, even the soppiest Beagle will be transformed into a hunting machine, picking up and holding the scent of any wild creature. They will follow the trail until it ends, usually being deaf to all entreaties. Then, the moment he gets home, he'll find the most comfortable chair, lie on it upside-down, and invite the family to tickle his tummy.

Special considerations
The garden needs to be fenced with Colditz in mind, as Beagles can be great escape artists. They dislike being left on their own.

Like this?
Check out these alternatives:

- Basenji
- Basset Hound
- Bloodhound
- Hamiltonstövare
- Petit Basset Griffon Vendeen

Vital statistics

Height:	33-40 cms
Weight:	13.5-16 kgs
Exercise:	●●○○○
Grooming:	●○○○○
Noise:	●●○○○
Food bill:	£4 per week

Country of origin:	Britain
Original function:	Hunting hares in packs
Availability:	Easy

Colours:	Any recognised hound colour. No liver. The tip of the tail must be white
Coat type:	Weather-proof, short and dense
Coat care:	A daily two-minute brush with a hound glove

Health

Average life span:	14 years
Hereditary disorders:	Parents and pups should be eye-tested. Test available for blood disorders. Some heart problems
Hip dysplasia:	23 (breed mean score)

Suitability

Exercise:	As much as you can give, then more
Ease of training:	Not easy
Temperament with children:	Extremely good, but children must learn to respect dogs and not treat them like toys
With dogs?	Good
With cats?	Okay with 'own', less tolerant of others
Town or country dog?	Country
Would he happily live in a flat or apartment?	If it has a garden and he has sufficient mental and physical stimulation
Natural guard dog?	No, but most will warn of intruders
Attitude to strangers?	Friendly

Want to know more?

Breed advice: Joan Lennard 0845 456 8334
Breed rescue: Beagle Welfare www.beagleadvice.org.uk

Character sketch

Beardies are variously described as fun-loving clowns, serious, madcap, affectionate, highly intelligent and almost telepathically attuned to their owners.

An untrained Beardie is abominable, however! Without guidance, they are rowdy, hyperactive, and, because they have more than their fair share of brains, they will devise ways to drive their owner to a point of lunacy.

For the right person, able to give them the training, exercise and mental stimulation they need, it's all worth it. The Beardie is an adorable companion who cares devoutly for his family.

Special considerations
This breed entails an enormous grooming commitment. Needs kind, regular training, things to do and think about, and room to run and play.

Like this?
Check out these alternatives:

- Briard
- Border Collie
- Deerhound
- Old English Sheepdog
- Tibetan Terrier

History

The Bearded Collie is probably the oldest of our native sheepdog breeds and has been variously known as the Highland Collie, the Scottish Bearded and the Hairy Mouthed Collie. These days, it is affectionately known as the Beardie.

Shepherds in the Scottish Highlands needed a particularly robust dog: the terrain was harsh, the weather severe and wolves still roamed the Highlands as late as the 1700s. Even the sheep were reputed to be more aggressive than the Lowland flocks! It is from these robust, intelligent, well-coated dogs that the Beardie was developed.

Vital statistics

Height:	51-56 cms
Weight:	18-25 kgs
Exercise:	●●●●
Grooming:	●●●●●
Noise:	●●●●
Food bill:	£6 per week

Country of origin:	Scotland, with European influence
Original function:	Sheepdog and cattle drover
Availability:	Fairly easy
Colours:	Born black, brown, fawn or blue with white markings. Sometimes tri-coloured. The coat usually pales as the dog gets older, but rarely some stay dark
Coat type:	Long, harsh outercoat, soft undercoat
Coat care:	Needs daily combing

Health

Average life span:	14 years
Hereditary disorders:	Eye-test parents. Autoimmune problems emerging
Hip dysplasia:	11 (breed mean score)

Suitability

Exercise:	Loves it - needs a good amount to remain healthy
Ease of training:	Easy
Temperament with children:	Excellent
With dogs?	Very good
With cats?	Will make good friends if introduced properly
Town or country dog?	Prefers country but is adaptable
Would he happily live in a flat or apartment?	Not recommended
Natural guard dog?	No, but will warn you of strangers
Attitude to strangers?	Friendly

Want to know more?

Breed advice: Margaret Fletcher 01438 353962; Belinda Steer 01344 453170
Breed rescue: Bob & Edna Manning 020 8303 8343; Sue Nicholls-Ward 01609 882574

Character sketch

If you want to be the proud owner of a dog that will stop traffic and soften the hardest of hearts, get a Bedlington. If you want a dog that will give the Japanese bullet train a run for its money, get a Bedlington. If you want a dog that will snooze away its days, fetch your slippers and accompany you into gentle retirement, *don't* get a Bedlington. This dog in lamb's clothing is full of spirit and sporting instincts. He's a good family companion, who is affectionate and quiet by nature. He likes to live close to his owners, and dislikes being left alone.

Special considerations
Needs to be treated with dignity; harshness is counterproductive. Must be exercised regularly and not allowed to get fat.

History

The Bedlington came about as a result of crosses between various terriers and possibly Whippets. He is closely related to the Dandie Dinmont and there is much debate on which came first. What's likely is that litters contained both long and short-legged puppies, and these were separated out and two distinct strains eventually evolved. The Bedlington grew up in the north-east and was favoured by miners, who admired his ability to control vermin in the coal pits. Bedlingtons were also used by poachers - which is why they were occasionally known as Gypsy dogs - but they were equally favoured by the landed gentry for their hunting skills.

Like this?
Check out these alternatives:

- Dandie Dinmont
- Poodle
- Irish Water Spaniel
- Curly Coated Retriever
- Belgian Shepherd Dog (Laekenois)

Vital statistics

Height:	41 cms
Weight:	Around 10 kgs
Exercise:	●●○○
Grooming:	●●●○
Noise:	●○○○
Food bill:	£4 per week on average

Country of origin:	Northern England
Original function:	Vermin Control
Availability:	Difficult

Colours:	Blue, liver, or sandy, with or without tan
Coat type:	Thick and 'linty'
Coat care:	Debris can be accumulated after a walk, so regular combing is needed. Coat needs to be cut every six to eight weeks to prevent matting

Health

Average life span:	13 years
Hereditary disorders:	Parents and puppies should be eye-tested and parents should have had a DNA test for copper toxicosis
Hip dysplasia:	13 (breed mean score)

Suitability

Exercise:	As much as you can give, but at least two good walks a day
Ease of training:	Moderate
Temperament with children:	Very good
With dogs?	Dominant with own breed
With cats?	Okay with own, watch it with others
Town or country dog?	Either, but probably prefers country
Would he happily live in a flat or apartment?	Yes, with sufficient exercise
Natural guard dog?	No
Attitude to strangers?	Friendly

Want to know more?

Breed advice: Mrs A M Emsley 01274 788773
Breed rescue: National Bedlington Terrier Rescue, Sheila Baldwin 01493 748981

History

Sheepdogs emerged across northern Europe in the 15th century, but the BSD is very much its own dog. BSDs herded and guarded flocks of sheep and they also worked as draught dogs, although stockier dogs were more commonly used for cart pulling. By the end of the 19th century, the BSD had become rare in Belgium, partly because they were replaced by collies, but also because sheep farming was in decline. The Club de Chien de Berger Belge (The Belgian Shepherd Dog Club) was founded in 1891 to rescue the breed from extinction. A standard was developed in 1892 and the four types of BSD were recognised.

Character sketch

Not a breed for everyone. BSDs are big dogs - both in size and character. They are also very active, wanting to be occupied all the time and the BSD is virtually inexhaustible. Belgian Shepherds are always on sentry duty, with their acute senses recognising anything unusual and making preparations to deal with it. Socialisation is a must, therefore.

Trained with care and understanding, the Belgian Shepherd Dog is an even-tempered, biddable, energetic, and fun dog. They love to be close to their owners, and are very affectionate and caring.

Special considerations
These dogs are big-time moulters! Keep them well groomed when they are shedding.

There are four types of Belgian Shepherd Dog each with a distinctive coat type: the Groenendael (left) and Tervueren (above top) have an abundant, medium-harsh topcoat and an extremely dense undercoat. The Laekenois (above centre) has a harsh, wiry, dry coat. The Malinois (above bottom) has a thick, firm, close-lying topcoat with a woolly undercoat.

Vital statistics

Height:	56-61 cms
Weight:	20.5-25 kgs
Exercise:	●●●●
Grooming:	●●○○
Noise:	●●●○
Food bill:	£9 per week on average

Country of origin:	Belgium
Original function:	Sheepdog and guard
Availability:	Moderate

Colours:	Groenendael, always black. Laekenois: reddish fawn with black shading. Tervueren/Malinois: all shades of red, fawn, or grey with black overlay
Coat care:	A brush through once or twice a week, more often if muddy

Health

Average life span:	13 years
Hereditary disorders:	Epilepsy, eye-test parents
Hip dysplasia:	9-11 (breed mean score) depending on variety

Suitability

Exercise:	The BSD needs around two-and-a-half hours' exercise each day, to include plenty of free-running
Ease of training:	Very easy
Temperament with children	Good, provided children treat them with respect
With dogs?	Usually good
With cats?	Okay with own; be careful with others
Town or country dog?	Country
Would he happily live in a flat or apartment?	Only if plenty of exercise is offered
Natural guard dog?	Very much so
Attitude to strangers?	Suspicious

Want to know more?

Breed advice: Pamela Davies 01202 623767; Janet Weller 01684 773423; Chris King 0121 706 6944
Breed rescue: Margaret Pretton 01159 447145; Debbie Lloyd 01384 221612

Bernese Mountain Dog

○ History

The Bernese is the best known of the four Swiss mountain dogs. The Bernese and the Greater Swiss Mountain dog developed in the valley regions, while the slightly smaller and nimbler Appenzeller and Entelbucher worked higher up in the mountains. The ancestors of the Bernese worked as all-purpose farm dogs from the Middle Ages, guarding cattle, being alert to danger, and keeping an eye on things in the remote farmsteads that characterise this Alpine region.

Around 1850, cheese production emerged as an important part of the economy in Bern. This added a new task to the list of chores carried out by Swiss mountain dogs: pulling carts of milk to market. This poor man's horse was also used by butchers, toolmakers and other traders, but it was their close association with the burgeoning dairy industry that led to the nickname 'cheesery dogs'.

Special considerations
Not keen on heat. A high-maintenance dog that needs space, human companionship and mental stimulation. Must not be allowed to get fat!

Like this?
Check out these alternatives:

- Leonberger
- Newfoundland
- Rottweiler
- St Bernard

○ Character sketch

When visiting a litter, realise that the adorable bundles of fur will be double the size in three months' time and those cute little tails will never stop wagging and will become more powerful with growth! The affectionate Bernese loves company and can be a great escape artist: a secure garden with at least a 6ft fence is a must.

They shed their thick coats, so a good vacuum cleaner is essential, as is the ability to cope with the odd hair in your dinner!

They can be stubborn and boisterous. It is far easier to train a small pup than a huge 50 kg dog, so it is crucial to commence training early.

○ Vital statistics

Height:	58-70 cms
Weight:	30-60 kgs
Exercise:	●●●○
Grooming:	●●●○
Noise:	●●○○
Food bill:	£10-£12 per week

Country of origin:	Switzerland
Original function:	General farm dog
Availability:	Moderate
Colours:	Black with reddish-brown on cheeks, legs, chest and above the eyes. White blaze on head, white markings on chest
Coat type:	A good undercoat, with a silky, wavy topcoat with a bright, natural sheen
Coat care:	Thorough combing three times a week

○ Health

Average life span:	8 years
Hereditary disorders:	Elbow dysplasia and a DNA test available for blood clotting disorder
Hip dysplasia:	15 (breed mean score)

○ Suitability

Exercise:	Two good walks a day, with free-running and play
Ease of training:	Fairly straightforward, though some can have a stubborn streak
Temperament with children:	Excellent with respectful children
With dogs?	Very good generally
With cats?	Usually non-aggressive
Town or country dog?	Either
Would he happily live in a flat or apartment?	If large enough - he needs plenty of space
Natural guard dog?	A good watchdog
Attitude to strangers?	Initially suspicious; will bark at strangers

Want to know more?

Breed advice: Helen Davenport-Willis 01670 590772
Breed rescue: Mrs Jude Simonds 01787 371940

Character sketch

The Bichon's gentle looks belie his energetic nature - he is a powerhouse of activity. These dogs are always happy to join in any family activity and hate to be alone.

Bichons are lavish in their affection and expect the same in return; if they are rejected coldly, they are prone to sulking. Although they are highly intelligent, they are strangely stubborn if they don't want to do something.

Above all, he'll make you laugh and keep you happy when you least feel like it. All these things, plus a gentle temperament, make him an excellent companion.

Special considerations

The coat is high-maintenance. If an owner cannot do the necessary hairdressing, the dog should be taken to the grooming parlour every six to eight weeks.

Like this?
Check out these alternatives:

- Bolognese • Maltese • Havanese

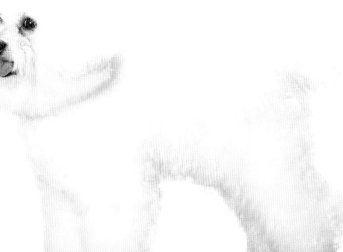

History

'Bichon' means 'small dog' in French and is also a term of endearment. 'Bichonner' means 'to groom' or 'to get dolled up'. 'Frise' means 'curly'. But, despite its name, the Bichon Frise isn't French at all. His ancestors came from the Canary Islands. It's thought that some kind of small, white, fluffy pooch was taken from Mediterranean islands in the 15th century by Spanish sailors, who traded the dogs across the Spanish empire, even as far as Cuba. These dogs are probably the ancestors of the Maltese, the Bolognese, the Havanese and, of course, the Bichon Frise, which was known for many years as the Bichon Tenerife, after its native homeland. These charming dogs became fashionable across Europe, especially France, and were often exchanged as gifts between royal and noble folk. Henry III (King of France 1574-1589), famously wore a basket round his neck in which he kept several bundles of tiny, curly canines.

Vital statistics

Height:	23-28 cms
Weight:	4.5-5.5 kgs
Exercise:	●○○○
Grooming:	●●●●
Noise:	●●●○
Food bill:	£3 per week

Country of origin:	Mediterranean area
Original function:	Companion
Availability:	Moderate
Colours:	White
Coat type:	Soft, with corkscrew curls
Coat care:	Daily brush and comb keeps the coat clean and tangle-free. Bath frequently, since there can be skin problems that need to be treated rapidly

Health

Average life span:	14 years
Hereditary disorders:	Parents should be eye-tested Patella luxation
Hip dysplasia:	10 (breed mean score)

Suitability

Exercise:	Do not require an enormous amount, but they love to go out, and will run and walk as much as the owner can manage
Ease of training:	Generally good
Temperament with children:	Good, provided children respect the dog
With dogs?	Excellent
With cats?	Very good
Town or country dog?	Either
Would he happily live in a flat or apartment?	Yes, provided he's given adequate mental stimulation
Natural guard dog?	Will give a warning bark
Attitude to strangers?	Friendly

Want to know more?

Breed advice: Doreen Harvey 01483 421959; Margaret Hoad 01323 764818
Breed rescue: Mr & Mrs Parrington 01524 771187; Helen Banfield 01753 735778

History

In most of Europe, Bloodhounds are called St Hubert Hounds. Hubert was a medieval nobleman with a passion for hunting in the Ardennes region of northern Europe. Legend has it that he had a vision while out hunting, which prompted him to renounce earthly delights and join a monastery. He did not, however, give up his dogs, and continued to breed his beloved hounds. When he died in 727 AD, the tradition was continued by other monks in the monastery, who gave the breed Hubert's name. The monks gave puppies as gifts to the king of France, who passed them on to his favourite nobles. The St Hubert's reputation as a steadfast, indefatigable hound quickly spread.

The incredible tracking abilities of these dogs were quickly put to use to track down thieves, poachers, marauders, eloping lovers and the like.

Character sketch

The Bloodhound is easygoing, humorous and affectionate. He adores the company of humans. But he is not a suitable pet for everyone, requiring long and interesting walks when adult.

If you can offer what the Bloodhound needs - space and exercise - he'll be a delightful house-pet and a most interesting companion, but do remember that when he gets his nose on a scent, he can suddenly develop hound deafness when you want him back!

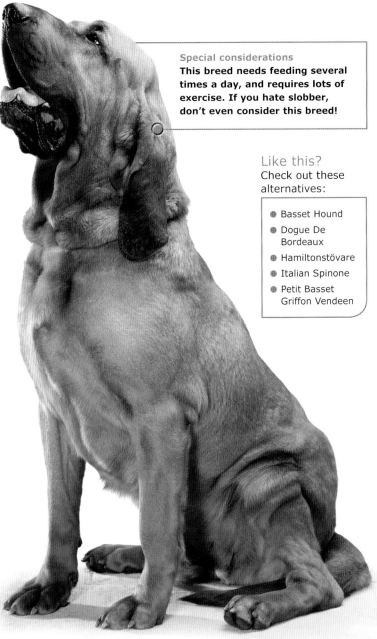

Special considerations
This breed needs feeding several times a day, and requires lots of exercise. If you hate slobber, don't even consider this breed!

Like this?
Check out these alternatives:

- Basset Hound
- Dogue De Bordeaux
- Hamiltonstövare
- Italian Spinone
- Petit Basset Griffon Vendeen

Vital statistics

Height:	58-69 cms
Weight:	36-50 kgs
Exercise:	●●●●
Grooming:	●●○○
Noise:	●●○○
Food bill:	£15-£20 per week

Country of origin:	France
Original function:	Hunting
Availability:	Difficult

Colours:	Black and tan, liver and tan, and red. White speckles and small white patch on the chest, feet and tail tip permissible
Coat type:	Velvety smooth, short and weatherproof
Coat care:	A twice-weekly brush and comb with a hound glove

Health

Average life span:	7 years
Hereditary disorders:	Parents and pups should be eye-tested. Torsion.
Hip dysplasia:	20 (breed mean score)

Suitability

Exercise:	Significant! Long, interesting walks needed
Ease of training:	Moderate
Temperament with children:	Really good
With dogs?	No problems; this is a very sociable hound
With cats?	Friendly with his 'own' family cat; not quick enough to catch others
Town or country dog?	Country
Would he happily live in a flat or apartment?	No, he needs space and exercise
Natural guard dog?	No
Attitude to strangers?	Friendly

Want to know more?

Breed advice: Mrs S Emrys-Jones 01637 880443
Breed rescue: Debra Pownall 01925 730606

History

By the first millennium BC there was a thriving trade across the near east and southern Europe in luxurious fabrics, exotic spices, precious metals and small dogs. These petit pooches had no particular purpose beyond being attractive and affectionate.

The Bolognese is closely related to other toy breeds with connections to far-flung corners of ancient empires. The Bichon Frise, the Maltese, the Havanese and the Coton de Tulear are probably all related and all came about because some adventurous sailors a long time ago took off in search of a lucrative sale.

This particular variety of small, white, curly-coated dog has become associated with the Italian city of Bologna. This is not to say that the Bolognese is, strictly speaking, an Italian native. The breed's ancestors had become well established in France during the 16th century, when they were popular with the French aristocracy. Following a series of religious wars that caused havoc in France, the breeding of these dogs switched to Bologna.

Like this?
Check out these alternatives:

- Bichon Frise
- Maltese
- Havanese

Character sketch

Bolognese hate being left alone and will become unhappy if left out of family activities. They can become very attached to one person and will follow them like a shadow. Generally, they like children, but they are not hyperactive with them; they enjoy gentle play, so children should be trained not to be rough.

A properly trained and loved Bolognese will bring happiness into a home. These happy little dogs are particularly appreciated by the young and the very old, simply because they are so gentle and easy to handle.

Special considerations
This dog is miserable when left alone. Grooming must be ongoing - any neglect will cause suffering.

Vital statistics

Height:	25.5-30.5 cms
Weight:	4 kgs
Exercise:	●○○○
Grooming:	●●●●
Noise:	●●●○
Food bill:	£5 per week

Country of origin:	Italy
Original function:	Companion
Availability:	Difficult

Colours:	White
Coat type:	Flocked - meaning a natural-looking coat that falls in soft ringlets
Coat care:	A thorough comb through at least every other day is essential to avoid matting

Health

Average life span:	11 years
Hereditary disorders:	No problems known to breeders
Hip dysplasia:	Insufficient numbers have been tested

Suitability

Exercise:	When fully grown, a minimum of two 20-minute walks a day, plus plenty of quality play
Ease of training:	Moderate
Temperament with children:	Excellent with well-behaved, sensible children
With dogs?	Good
With cats?	Good, if brought up with them
Town or country dog?	Either
Would he happily live in a flat or apartment?	Yes, if adequately exercised
Natural guard dog?	No, but they do bark to alert you
Attitude to strangers?	Reserved until they get to know you - and then friendly and loving

Want to know more?

Breed advice: Jill Richards 01773 716021
Breed rescue: Martin & Gina Taylor 01452 536069

Border Collie

Character sketch

The Border Collie is loving and affectionate, but is not the ideal pet for every household - they need space and occupation! They are so intelligent, they need a great deal of mental stimulation, otherwise they can get restless and become destructive.

A study carried out in 1972 claimed the breed has the problem-solving ability of a 12-year-old child! If they can't work, they will need plenty of exercise, and they are ideally suited to agility and flyball.

If you give them enough to do in a country environment and surround them with active people, they make wonderful companions.

Special considerations
This breed needs to be mentally occupied. Boredom can make them destructive and edgy.

History

The Border Collie was not admitted into the Kennel Club until 1976. Before this, the collie was in the hands of hardy sheep farmers who couldn't give a fig about physical appearance. They wanted a dog who could do the job - and that was the end of the matter.

Humans have relied on sheepdogs ever since sheep were first domesticated. But dogs were used mainly for guarding rather than herding, which is why many of the world's sheepdog breeds are large and muscular. By the 13th century, such guard dogs were an essential part of Britain's booming wool industry.

However, these dogs became redundant in the 15th century when wolves became extinct in England (later in Scotland). With no large predators, shepherds no longer needed a security force. The eventual result was a slight, nimble sheepdog, with more brains than brawn.

Like this?
Check out these alternatives:

- Bearded Collie
- Bernese Mountain Dog
- Collie (Rough)
- Australian Shepherd Dog

Vital statistics

Height:	Around 53 cms
Weight:	20 kgs
Exercise:	●●●●
Grooming:	●●○○
Noise:	●●●○
Food bill:	About £6 per week

Country of origin:	Border country (Scotland and Wales)
Original function:	Working sheepdog and guard
Availability:	Easy

Colours:	Common colours include: black and white, blue and white, red and white, tri-colour, blue merle and red merle
Coat type:	Two types - smooth or moderately long with a weather-resistant, double coat
Coat care:	A daily brush and comb

Health

Average life span:	14 years
Hereditary disorders:	Eye-test parents and pups. Some deafness. DNA test available for metabolic disorder
Hip dysplasia:	13 (breed mean score)

Suitability

Exercise:	Significant - but mental stimulation is just as important
Ease of training:	Easy, with the right training
Temperament with children:	Good with 'trained' children but supervision essential as he may herd them
With dogs?	Pretty good
With cats?	Okay with his own cats if trained and socialised well; may chase others
Town or country dog?	Country
Would he happily live in a flat or apartment?	No
Natural guard dog?	Will usually warn of strangers
Attitude to strangers?	Wary

Want to know more?

Breed advice: Justine Gladwell-Hunt 01208 831778; Erica Down 01228 791382
Breed Rescue: Border Collie Trust GB 0871 560 2282; Val Phillips 01883 624513

Special considerations
As well as needing plenty of exercise (when adult), they also need lots of play-time with their owners.

Like this?
Check out these alternatives:

- Cairn Terrier
- Irish Terrier
- Norfolk Terrier
- Parson Russell Terrier
- Welsh Terrier

History

His origins lie in the remote, hilly border regions between England and Scotland. Several different types of terrier emerged from this part of the country: the Dandie Dinmont, Lakeland and Bedlington.

Although paintings and illustrations indicate that a Border Terrier-type dog was known in Westmoreland and Cumberland during the 18th century, the breed did not become fixed until the middle of the 19th century and was not recognised by the Kennel Club until 1920.

Border Terriers were originally kept as ratters and were also worked alongside packs of Foxhounds. They were often kennelled with hounds, which made them less argumentative with other dogs than some terrier breeds.

Character sketch

An affectionate, energetic, charming and playful companion, popular with all ages. He retains his hunting instincts, but is affable in the house.

The Border Terrier quite likes children, although they must show him respect; if they overstep the mark with rough play, he will indicate his displeasure. With kind, responsible children, he is a great companion.

While the Border Terrier can and does make a lovely family pet, he should not be taken on lightly or without the potential owners being aware of his working traits and habits. Drawbacks can be their determination to dig their way out of a garden or attack the neighbourhood cat. If you are prepared to share your life with a true terrier-like terrier, then you will not be disappointed in the Border Terrier.

Vital statistics

Height:	35.5 cms
Weight:	5-7 kgs
Exercise:	●●○○
Grooming:	●●●○
Noise:	●●○○
Food bill:	£8 per week

Country of origin:	Scotland and England
Original function:	Vermin control
Availability:	Moderate

Colours:	Red, wheaten, grizzle and tan, or blue and tan
Coat type:	Harsh, dense outer coat, thick, soft undercoat. Thick pelt (skin)
Coat care:	Daily brush and comb, plus top coat should be handstripped twice a year

Health

Average life span:	14 years
Hereditary disorders:	Parents should be eye-tested
Hip dysplasia:	14 (breed mean score)

Suitability

Exercise:	Needs a good deal of physical and mental stimulation
Ease of training:	Moderate. Brainy but can be stubborn!
Temperament with children:	Good, if treated respectfully
With dogs?	Can become dog-aggressive if they have not been socialised from an early age
With cats?	Good, if raised with them from young, but cats can still be seen as 'prey'
Town or country dog?	Either, though he prefers country life
Would he happily live in a flat or apartment?	Only with sufficient exercise
Natural guard dog?	Will warn - then befriend the intruder!
Attitude to strangers?	Initially suspicious, then friendly

Want to know more?

Breed advice: Christine Sneddon 01204 880465; Susan Williams 01706 623660; Betty A Judge 01793 783297
Breed rescue: Lesley Smith-Fenton 01388 537718

Borzoi

Character sketch

Courageous and fast, the Borzoi is a sensitive dog with an independent, stubborn streak. Loyal and affectionate, this is a real canine conversation-stopper! His whole demeanour is so aristocratic and superior. Maybe because he is aloof and standoffish, he is not the breed for everyone.

By their very nature, they are hunters, and they need early training, particularly with recall. Exercise is important to him - he is born to run.

For such a big dog he takes up remarkably little space and is quiet by nature. In all, he makes a most elegant addition to a family and will prove to be a good and faithful friend.

Like this?
Check out these alternatives:

- Afghan Hound
- Deerhound
- Greyhound
- Whippet

History

These most majestic of sighthounds have a noble heritage to match their distinguished appearance. Inevitably, they found themselves on the losing side during the Russian Revolution. These aristocratic dogs only narrowly escaped extinction with the ill-fated Russian monarchy.

The story of the Russian Wolfhound, though, begins long before. They were already well established in Russia by 1650. It's thought that sighthounds arrived in Russia from Central Asia, possibly during the Tartar invasions. They were later crossed with native breeds to produce a hardier hound. Borzois worked in groups of three and were trained to corner a wolf, which would then be killed or captured by a huntsman.

The name 'Borzoi' comes from a Russian word meaning 'swift'.

Special considerations
Early socialisation is a must! Patience is the key when training.

Vital statistics

Height:	68-74 cms
Weight:	27-45 kgs
Exercise:	●●○○
Grooming:	●●○○
Noise:	●○○○
Food bill:	£7 per week

Country of origin:	Russia
Original function:	Hunting wolves
Availability:	Difficult

Colours:	Any colour acceptable
Coat type:	Silky, flat, wavy or rather curly, but never woolly
Coat care:	A good brush through is necessary twice a week; more if living in country conditions

Health

Average life span:	11 years
Hereditary disorders:	No problems known to breeders
Hip dysplasia:	Insufficient numbers have been tested

Suitability

Exercise:	Needs a good gallop and a walk daily, though he is usually happy to have occasional lazy days
Ease of training:	Moderately easy, with patience and persistence
Temperament with children:	Okay, if socialised and if the children are respectful
With dogs?	Okay, unless challenged
With cats?	Very iffy
Town or country dog?	Prefers country life
Would he happily live in a flat or apartment?	No
Natural guard dog?	No
Attitude to strangers?	Can be suspicious

Want to know more?

Breed advice: Christine Spencer 01769 580578
Breed rescue: Sue Simon 0208 684 3958

History

The Boston Terrier, like most human Americans, is the product of immigrant stock. The first Boston, in fact, may well have been Liverpudlian. A dog called Judge - a cross between a Bulldog and an English White Terrier - made the journey across the Atlantic, where it became known as Hooper's Judge, when a man from Boston called Robert Hooper bought the dog around 1875.

   Although the Boston Terrier was to become known as the American Gentleman because of his dapper appearance and polished manners, the breed's heritage actually lies in the seedy world of the rat pit and the dog fight.

   Formally declared the state dog of Massachusetts in 1979, the Boston has also been the official mascot of Boston University since 1922.

Character sketch

One of their most endearing characteristics is their intelligence. They are quick to learn what is wanted from them in domestic situations; they also quickly learn to do the tricks that are so popular with children.

   It is said they have the liveliness of a terrier but with the noble attitude of the Mastiff. They have genes from both, but so far back to have been largely negated. They do not seek altercations with other dogs, but if they are attacked, they will remember how to defend themselves.

   A happy dog, the Boston Terrier is full of fun and surprises, and is simply a joy to own.

Like this?
Check out these alternatives:

- Boxer
- Bulldog
- Pug

Special considerations
The Boston's eyes are vulnerable, so keep him away from undergrowth where twigs and briars can pose a danger.

Vital statistics

Height:	30.5-35.5 cms
Weight:	Lightweight (under 7 kgs), middleweight (7-9 kgs); heavyweight (9-11.5 kgs)
Exercise:	●●○○
Grooming:	●○○○
Noise:	●○○○
Food bill:	£6 per week

Country of origin:	America
Original function:	Yard dog vermin killer
Availability:	Difficult
Colours:	Brindle with white markings preferred, black with white markings acceptable
Coat type:	Short and smooth, with a fine texture
Coat care:	A weekly gloss over with a hound glove

Health

Average life span:	12 years
Hereditary disorders:	Parents and pups should be eye-tested. Patella luxation
Hip dysplasia:	Insufficient numbers have been tested

Suitability

Exercise:	Two 20-minute walks a day will suffice, with play in the garden
Ease of training:	Straightforward - these dogs are smart!
Temperament with children:	Excellent with older, respectful children
With dogs?	Generally, excellent - though some males can be a bit assertive
With cats?	Likely to chase any non-family cats
Town or country dog?	Either
Would he happily live in a flat or apartment?	Yes, provided he's sufficiently exercised and mentally stimulated
Natural guard dog?	No, but they are alert to strange sounds
Attitude to strangers?	Fairly friendly

Want to know more?

Breed advice: Mrs V Tanner 01892 652 095; Mrs Metcalfe 01942 511104
Breed rescue: Mrs V Tanner 01892 652 095

History

The Boxer that we know today is relatively modern - the breed standard was first established in his native Germany in 1905 - but his origins are ancient. It's thought that the Boxer came about through a happy mingling of Mastiffs with Bulldog-type dogs. The Mastiff probably arrived in Europe around the 6th century. One branch of the Mastiff family tree turned eventually into the Boxer.

By the 16th century, a Boxer-like dog known as the Bullenbeisser (literally, bull-biter) had become a familiar sight in Germany.

Gradually, our Boxer prototype moved into different fields of work as the forests were hacked back and the wild boar hunted to near extinction. They were used for bull-baiting as well as cattle-herding, draught work, and general farm-guarding duties.

The breed's dependability, loyalty and courage were exploited by the German army in both World Wars, and the Boxer was also one of the first breeds to be trained for use by the German police force.

Character sketch

Boxers are bouncing, boisterous, rambunctious and clown-like. A Boxer does nothing by half - he runs like a Greyhound, jumps like a gazelle, and will eat every meal as if he's never been fed before.

He is very affectionate, thriving on all the attention he can get, and adores family life. A Boxer has no idea how big he is and considers himself a lap dog!

Boxers are very intelligent and will learn quickly - but that doesn't mean they are always obedient. If there's fun to be had by ignoring you, and he isn't sufficiently motivated to avoid the temptation, then you've had it!

Like this?
Check out these alternatives:

- Boston Terrier
- Bulldog
- Rottweiler
- Staffordshire Bull Terrier

Special considerations

The Boxer loves company. Males can be dominant if untrained, so they need firm but fair handling. Care must be taken when grooming, as they have sensitive, thin skin.

Vital statistics

Height:	53-63 cms
Weight:	25-32 kgs
Exercise:	●●●●
Grooming:	●●○○
Noise:	●○○○
Food bill:	£6 per week

Country of origin:	Germany
Original function:	Guarding and security
Availability:	Easy

Colours:	Fawn or brindle. White on the coat is not to exceed one-third of it
Coat type:	Short and smooth
Coat care:	Regular (weekly) gentle brushing with a soft brush

Health

Average life span:	12 years
Hereditary disorders:	Serious heart problems. Only buy from heart-tested parents. Some deafness in white dogs
Hip dysplasia:	16 (breed mean score)

Suitability

Exercise:	Two good walks a day, including some free-running
Ease of training:	Quite easy
Temperament with children:	Very good
With dogs?	Very good
With cats?	Good
Town or country dog?	Either, but probably prefers the country
Would he happily live in a flat or apartment?	Yes, with appropriate exercise
Natural guard dog?	Yes
Attitude to strangers?	Suspicious

Want to know more?

Breed advice: Michael Gordon 01205 362647; Blanka Warner 020 8318 3400
Breed rescue: Home Counties Boxer Welfare, Ann 01525 240288 and Rosemary 01747 822345

Character sketch

The Briard is not a dog for everyone: he's big, highly intelligent and sensitive. Right from the start, an owner must work with the dog, but the end product will be an extraordinary pet of whom the whole family will be proud. It is not for nothing that the breed is known as 'a heart wrapped in fur'.

The Briard loves his family dearly and will guard them with his life. A well-educated Briard is an absolute joy to own; he is a real home-loving dog that hates to be deprived of human company.

Like this?
Check out these alternatives:

- Bearded Collie
- Old English Sheepdog
- Tibetan Terrier

History

In France he is known as the Berger de Brie - because he herded sheep on the plains in the Brie region, near Paris. The Briard is closely related to the Beauceron - known as the Berger de Beauce in France - which comes from the same region. Indeed, the two dogs were once considered as short- and long-haired versions of the same breed and were not officially recognised as distinct until 1896.

The Briard could be the result of crosses between the Beauceron and the Barbet, an old breed that is a cousin of the Poodle.

Briards were used to guard flocks from wolves and poachers and as general guard and tracking dogs. During the First World War, they carried equipment, patrolled the front lines, and located injured soldiers. Briards have since been used as police dogs and guide dogs for the blind.

> **Special considerations**
> To avoid bloat, his food should be divided into four to five portions per day; the breeder should give you bloat advice, too.

Vital statistics

Height:	58-69 cms
Weight:	30 kgs
Exercise:	●●●●
Grooming:	●●●●
Noise:	●●●○
Food bill:	£8 per week

Country of origin:	France
Original function:	Shepherd's dog, droving and security
Availability:	Difficult

Colours:	All black with scattered white hairs; all shades of fawn; slate grey
Coat type:	Fine, dense undercoat, long outercoat. Moustache, beard and eyebrows essential
Coat care:	A thorough brush and comb through at least three times a week

Health

Average life span:	14 years
Hereditary disorders:	Only buy from eye-tested parents
Hip dysplasia:	18 (breed mean score)

Suitability

Exercise:	A good deal when fully mature
Ease of training:	Okay with kind, patient training
Temperament with children:	Superb with respectful kids
With dogs?	Generally good; some males can be dominant with others
With cats?	No problem, if he's been socialised as a pup with them, and is introduced to them with care
Town or country dog?	Either, though he prefers country life
Would he happily live in a flat or apartment?	Only with adequate exercise
Natural guard dog?	Very much so
Attitude to strangers?	Initially suspicious

Want to know more?

Breed advice & rescue: Sheila Cann 01932 781578

History

The breed is derived from the ancient Molossus, the Mastiff-style dogs that originated in central Asia. They were big, aggressive dogs, which some tribes used as war dogs. They found their way to ancient Greece, and thence to Rome, where the Roman soldiers used them to great effect as war and defence dogs on their campaigns throughout Europe. The theory is that many dogs and puppies were left behind as the armies passed through, mixing with an area's local dogs.

For bull-baiting, special dogs were bred that were big enough, agile enough and game enough to bring a bull down. Bull baiting was banned in 1835, but there was another subsidiary sport - dog fighting. This required an extremely game and agile dog, and breeders turned their attention to breeding dogs specifically to fight. They required a lighter, smaller dog but with great jaw power, and these dogs were the probable forefathers of today's Bulldog.

Like this?
Check out these alternatives:

- Boxer
- Boston Terrier
- Bull Terrier
- Staffordshire Bull Terrier

Special considerations
Keep your dog cool, especially in a car, and never leave him in a vehicle. Do not exercise him in hot weather. Keep the muzzle, tail, wrinkles, and ears clean and dry.

Character sketch

Affable and laid-back, the Bulldog is a sociable pet. His grumpy look belies the fact that he is a fun dog and a natural clown. Nothing about his temperament betrays his sinister past; he never looks to quarrel, but if another dog forces him into a position where he must defend himself, he will acquit himself extremely well.

Bulldogs are most affectionate and loyal, wanting to be close to their human family most of their waking day.

Vital statistics

Height:	Around 40.5 cms
Weight:	23-25 kgs
Exercise:	●●○○
Grooming:	●●○○
Noise:	●○○○
Food bill:	£4 per week

Country of origin:	Britain
Original function:	Bull-baiting
Availability:	Difficult

Colours:	Whole colour or smut (whole colour with black mask or muzzle). Brindle, red, fawn, fallow, white, or white with any of these colours
Coat type:	Short and smooth
Coat care:	Daily brushing with a hound glove. The muzzle must be kept clean after feeding

Health

Average life span:	9 years
Hereditary disorders:	Deafness and heart problems; natural birth is impossible for many; check parents' breathing
Hip dysplasia:	45 (breed mean score)

Suitability

Exercise:	Two walks a day, plus play in the garden
Ease of training:	Not easy; needs patience
Temperament with children:	Very good
With dogs?	Good
With cats?	Excellent with his 'own'; with others, inquisitive but not aggressive
Town or country dog?	Either
Would he happily live in a flat or apartment?	Yes
Natural guard dog?	Not really, but will warn of intruders
Attitude to strangers?	Not suspicious

Want to know more?

Breed advice: Mrs M Mortham 01362 683639
Breed rescue: Bulldog Rescue 01730 810531

History

The Bull Terrier's ancestors were born into the dark and shadowy underworld of dimly lit taverns and backroom bars. The dog of choice in the bloody baiting arena had traditionally been the Bulldog, but the breed fell out of favour towards the end of the 18th century, when enthusiasm for baiting bears and bulls declined and dog fighting became increasingly popular.

The Bulldog was considered too slow, so they were crossed with terriers to produce a quicker, taller canine gladiator. These dogs were known as Bull-and-Terriers and they were highly prized for their speed and ferocity. These early crosses led to the development of both the Bull Terrier and the Staffordshire Bull Terrier.

Character sketch

The Bull Terrier is a highly intelligent, independent animal, who is able to act on his own initiative. From the onset, socialisation and training are essential, for he will be a hulk of muscle when adult.

If another dog challenges him, normally he'll ignore it; but if it becomes inevitable, he will defend himself. Always keep him on a lead unless in a safe, enclosed area, as this is a curious breed with no road sense. If he sees something interesting on the other side of the road, he is likely to go to investigate, ignoring the perils.

The Bull Terrier is a great companion and an exceptional family addition. A breed with humour - often described as a toddler in a dog suit!

Like this?
Check out these alternatives:

- Bulldog
- Boxer
- Staffordshire Bull Terrier

Special considerations
Bull Terriers must be kept very secure, as this breed is subject to theft. Ideally, get them tattooed in the ear, so that thieves can clearly see the dogs are identified.

Vital statistics

Height:	Most stand at around 56 cms
Weight:	32 kgs approximately
Exercise:	●●●○
Grooming:	●○○○
Noise:	●●○○
Food bill:	£8-£10 per week for an adult

Country of origin:	England
Original function:	'Gentleman's companion', vermin killer
Availability:	Easy

Colours:	White or coloured. For the latter, the colour should predominate. Brindle is preferred, or red, fawn, and tricolour
Coat type:	Harsh, short and flat
Coat care:	A weekly brush and polish with a hound glove

Health

Average life span:	12 years
Hereditary disorders:	Patella luxation; hereditary deafness; heart and kidney problems detected
Hip dysplasia:	7 (breed mean score)

Suitability

Exercise:	As much as possible when adult
Ease of training:	Persistent, kind training eventually pays off!
Temperament with children:	Superb with respectful children
With dogs?	Males can be dominant, particularly with their own breed
With cats?	With careful socialisation at puppyhood, usually okay. With others, watch it!
Town or country dog?	Either
Would he happily live in a flat or apartment?	Yes, if adequately exercised and mentally stimulated
Natural guard dog?	Quiet but observant
Attitude to strangers?	Friendly

Want to know more?

Breed advice: Juliet Shaw 01233 720340
Breed rescue: Linda McGregor 01923 232673

Cairn Terrier

History

The Cairn was not recognised by the Kennel Club until 1910, although it is one of Scotland's oldest terriers.

The Cairn gets its name from a Gaelic word for the mounds of stones that were traditionally piled up to mark graves, memorial sites, pathways and mountain tops. Terriers would have scrambled around cairns in search of prey (often badgers and foxes) on their hunting trips. These dogs were often worth a considerable amount of money. Indeed, James VI of Scotland deemed six terriers a worthy gift for the King of France.

Early Cairns were known by various other names, including the Skye Otter Terrier and the Short-haired Skye Terrier. After protracted wrangling with Skye Terrier enthusiasts, the short-haired version was officially named the Cairn Terrier in 1910 to prevent confusion between the two breeds. Both Cairn and Skye Terriers are thought to have originated on the Isle of Skye, and both are descended from very early terrier-type dogs.

The West Highland Terrier is also, in effect, a white Cairn. No wonder it took a while to separate the breeds and settle on names!

Like this?
Check out these alternatives:

- Dandie Dinmont Terrier
- Norfolk/Norwich Terrier
- Scottish Terrier
- West Highland White Terrier

Character sketch

A most loveable, mischievous, affectionate pet, these dogs are bundles of energy and have an inquisitiveness that is hard to match. They love nothing more than to run wildly around a garden, investigating everything. Cairns have such exuberant natures that they must be taught the house rules, so training is essential. Fortunately, they are intelligent and learn to be quite obedient, though, being terriers, they have a streak of independence.

Special considerations
Early socialisation and training are essential.

Vital statistics

Height:	28-31 cms
Weight:	6-7.5 kgs
Exercise:	●●○○
Grooming:	●●○○
Noise:	●●○○
Food bill:	£4 per week

Country of origin:	Scotland
Original function:	Vermin control
Availability:	Moderate

Colours:	Cream, wheaten, red, grey or nearly black
Coat type:	Weather-resistant, profuse, harsh outercoat, moderately close, soft undercoat
Coat care:	A brush through with a wide-toothed metal comb once or twice a week

Health

Average life span:	14 years
Hereditary disorders:	Eye-test parents and pups, liver shunt, DNA tests available for other problems
Hip dysplasia:	Insufficient numbers have been tested

Suitability

Exercise:	A couple of good walks a day is ideal
Ease of training:	Fairly good if kind and consistent
Temperament with children:	Very good, if treated with respect
With dogs?	Generally good, though males can be dominant sometimes
With cats?	Okay with their own; exercise great caution with others, though
Town or country dog?	Either, though he prefers the country
Would he happily live in a flat or apartment?	Yes, with adequate care and exercise
Natural guard dog?	He reacts well to strange noises
Attitude to strangers?	Friendly

Want to know more?

Breed advice: Deirdre Burnett 020 8670 6565; Sybil Berrecloth 01382 457601; Angela Osborn 01252 621523
Breed rescue: Mrs Chris Roberts 01283 712498

History

Comfort spaniels were popular in aristocratic homes on the continent in the 15th and 16th centuries. Charles I kept spaniels of all sizes, and legend goes that every spaniel in the land wept at his execution - but it was Charles II who grew particularly fond of the breed that would eventually bear his name. The Toy Spaniel Club was founded in 1855. Initially, different colour combinations were recognised as different breeds, but in 1903 the Kennel Club amalgamated them all under one breed standard: the King Charles Spaniel. By this time, though, the King Charles Spaniel had developed a shorter nose and the dome of the head had become more pronounced. American dog enthusiast Roswell Eldridge visited England in the 1920s and was disappointed to find that the traditional look of the breed had all but disappeared. He decided to recreate the dogs of old: in 1926, he offered a £25 prize at Crufts for five years running, which was to be awarded to the best "long-faced spaniels of the old type". The plan was successful and a new 'old' breed was born.

King Charles Spaniels

The Cavalier has a much rarer, older and often slightly smaller relative, which may be worth checking out. The Cavalier only dates back to 1945, but the King Charles can trace its roots to the 15th Century.

Like this?

Check out these alternatives:

- American Cocker Spaniel
- Cocker Spaniel
- Shih Tzu
- Tibetan Spaniel

Character sketch

One of the most tractable of all dog breeds, the Cavalier appeals to every age from children up to pensioners. Small enough to carry, he is docile, gentle and intelligent. He very quickly learns the ways and moods of his family and fits in like a close member of the household.

Special considerations

Be extra-vigilant to avoid puppy farmers/dealers, and buy only from reputable breeders who have done the relevant health tests.

Vital statistics

Height:	30.5-33 cms
Weight:	5.5 to 8 kgs
Exercise:	●●○○
Grooming:	●●○○
Noise:	●●○○
Food bill:	£5 per week for an adult

Country of origin:	England, with early European influence
Original function:	Comforter
Availability:	Easy
Colours:	Black and tan (whole black colour with tan markings), Blenheim (rich chestnut broken up with white), tricolour (black, white and tan), or ruby (rich red whole colour)
Coat type:	Long, fine and silky
Coat care:	A daily comb will prevent tangles

Health

Average life span:	11 years
Hereditary disorders:	Serious heart problems - only buy from heart-tested parents. Parents and pups should be eye-tested. Syringomyelia
Hip dysplasia:	16 (breed mean score)

Suitability

Exercise:	Half-hour walk twice a day, with plenty of play throughout the day
Ease of training:	Straightforward, they love to please
Temperament with children:	Good, but children must be respectful
With dogs?	No problems
With cats?	Good, if brought up with them
Town or country dog?	Either
Would he happily live in a flat or apartment?	Yes, if adequately exercised and mentally stimulated
Natural guard dog?	No, but he's very watchful
Attitude to strangers?	Friendly

Want to know more?

Breed advice: Mrs Bunting 01268 561374; Carol Fowler 01453 843944; Chris Knight 01636 626618
Breed rescue: Mrs J Pagan 01245 320488; Gillian Greenall 01548 580369

Chihuahua

History

From the Mexican state of Chihuahua, this tiny dog is closely associated with the Aztecs, who dominated the region for thousands of years until the Spanish conquest. Sculptures of small, bat-eared dogs dating back to the 5th century AD have been found in Mexico, leading many to conclude that the Chihuahua is one of the few breeds of dog to have emerged in the Americas.

The Aztecs certainly kept dogs for food in ancient times and dogs may have been used as scapegoats, taking the place of humans in sacrificial rites. Effigies of dogs and, in some cases, dog skeletons, have been found in human burial sites. It's believed that early Mexicans - much like the ancient Egyptians - buried animals with their owners to act as guides to the afterlife.

Special considerations
The Chihuahua must not be treated as a toy, especially by children. Teeth need regular attention.

Character sketch

The smallest of all breeds believes itself to be mightier than the mightiest. Woe betide a Bullmastiff who wants to mix with one of these zesty canines!
To their human family, Chihuahuas are all love and affection. They want to be with their loved ones for all activities and are frustrated if deprived of human company. It would be easy to mollycoddle so small a dog, but this should be avoided: Chihuahuas are real dogs, not toys, and they love to run and play in open spaces just like their big counterparts.

Like this?
Check out these alternatives:

- Miniature Pinscher
- Shih Tzu
- Yorkshire Terrier

Vital statistics

Height:	About 16.5-20.5 cms
Weight:	1.8-2.7 kgs
Exercise:	●○○○
Grooming:	●●○○
Noise:	●●○○
Food bill:	£3 per week

Country of origin:	Mexico
Original function:	Companion
Availability:	Moderate

Colours:	Any colour or mixture of colours - but never merle (dapple)
Coat type:	Smooth or long
Coat care:	A weekly brush and comb for both coats; the smooth type can be polished with a hound glove

Health

Average life span:	14 years
Hereditary disorders:	Patella luxation, heart murmurs. DNA test available for a blood disorder
Hip dysplasia:	Insufficient numbers have been tested

Suitability

Exercise:	Two 20-minute walks a day adequate
Ease of training:	Easy
Temperament with children:	Good with respectful children; but not wise to home them with young or boisterous youngsters, as the dogs can be injured easily
With dogs?	Not overly sociable; good with own breed
With cats?	Okay with 'own' cats if well socialised
Town or country dog?	Town, though he does enjoy the country
Would he happily live in a flat or apartment?	Yes, with adequate exercise and toilet breaks
Natural guard dog?	No, but he's watchful
Attitude to strangers?	Suspicious until introduced

Want to know more?

Breed advice: Margaret Greening 01249 783522; Jean Bright 01354 693535; Helen Davenport-Willis 01670 590772
Breed rescue: Pam Bungard 01273 413501

Special considerations

Needs daily brushing because he moults all the time - get a good vacuum cleaner! Can be stubborn, so needs early, patient training.

Character sketch

A big dog on short legs, the Clumber Spaniel is a docile fellow. His natural gentleness makes him ideal as a country family pet. He is highly intelligent and quickly learns what is expected of him, although he can be stubborn. He is really a country dog at heart, and likes to stroll rather than walk at speed.

This is a very affable, laidback dog, who is devoted to his family and has a special affinity with children.

Like this?
Check out these alternatives:

- American Cocker Spaniel
- English Springer Spaniel
- Cocker Spaniel
- Welsh Springer Spaniel

History

Some say that the Clumber Spaniel came to Britain as a refugee from the French Revolution. The Duc de Noailles was so worried that his prize dogs would become victims of the revolution that his spaniels were shipped to Britain and given to the second Duke of Newcastle for safe-keeping.

Others suggest that the Clumber Spaniel was developed in Britain from other breeds of spaniel, with perhaps a bit of Basset Hound thrown in.

Regardless, the Clumber Spaniel gained its name and reputation from Clumber Park, the historic seat of the Dukes of Newcastle, which is in Nottinghamshire.

Clumber Spaniels were popular gundogs on country estates and became a Royal Family tradition for several generations. Gradually, though, the Clumber lost ground to other, faster gundogs, notably the Springer Spaniel. The Cocker Spaniel was also eclipsed by the Springer on the shooting circuit but maintained popularity as a household pet. The same, alas, cannot be said of its dignified Clumber cousin.

Vital statistics

Height:	43-51 cms
Weight:	25-34 kgs
Exercise:	●●●○
Grooming:	●●●○
Noise:	●●●○
Food bill:	£7 per week for an adult

Country of origin:	England
Original function:	Flushing game
Availability:	Difficult

Colours:	Plain white body with lemon markings; orange markings permissible
Coat type:	Silky, close and straight
Coat care:	Daily grooming with a firm bristle brush

Health

Average life span:	10 years
Hereditary disorders:	Eyelash problem. DNA test available for a metabolic disorder
Hip dysplasia:	37 (breed mean score)

Suitability

Exercise:	Must have regular daily exercise as well as garden play
Ease of training:	Okay
Temperament with: children	Affable, gentle and laidback
With dogs?	No problems
With cats?	Generally okay; may chase
Town or country dog?	Country
Would he happily live in a flat or apartment?	No
Natural guard dog?	No
Attitude to strangers?	Friendly

Want to know more?

Breed advice: Carol Page 01489 589734
Breed rescue: Linda Lockett 01977 645422

Cocker Spaniel

Character sketch

Devoted to his owners, the Cocker is always anxious to please. He's bright and intelligent, and loves playing with children - providing they are as gentle with him as he is with them. He's easily taught and excels in games of seeking and retrieving. The breed is at its happiest when fully occupied, both physically and mentally, and owners should be prepared to give adequate exercise where the dog can demonstrate his incredible scenting powers. An ideal town or country pet, the Cocker is hardy, loving, intelligent, and, of course, merry!

History

A spaniel-type dog probably emerged in Spain around the 14th century and remained a firm favourite in royal courts across Europe for many generations. Small spaniels, known as 'comfort' or 'carpet' spaniels, made perfect household companions, while their larger cousins accompanied well-heeled masters on hunting expeditions. The working dogs were eventually divided into 'land' and 'water' spaniels.

The fine-tuning of different breeds of spaniel began in earnest in the 1800s when we find references to Cocker, Field, Springer, Sussex, Welsh and Devonshire Spaniels. Perhaps because of its small size, the field skills of the Cocker were eventually eclipsed by Springers and other gundogs, such as Labradors. Cockers lost the knack of pestering game birds and their sporting use gradually declined.

Special considerations

This breed needs to be kept occupied with games, agility, long country walks... anything to stimulate his mind. Ears need daily grooming.

Like this?
Check out these alternatives:

- American Cocker Spaniel
- Cavalier King Charles Spaniel
- English Springer Spaniel
- Welsh Springer Spaniel

Vital statistics

Height:	38-41 cms
Weight:	13-14.5 kgs
Exercise:	●●●○
Grooming:	●●●●
Noise:	●●○○
Food bill:	£5 per week

Country of origin:	Spain
Original function:	To flush and retrieve small game
Availability:	Easy

Colours:	About 20 combinations of whole/parti-colours
Coat type:	Flat, silky and well feathered
Coat care:	A daily brush and comb to keep the coat tangle-free

Health

Average life span:	12 years
Hereditary disorders:	Eye-test pups and parents. DNA test available for a kidney problem
Hip dysplasia:	14 (breed mean score)

Suitability

Exercise:	As much as possible. Consistent daily exercise is essential
Ease of training:	Easy
Temperament with children:	Good with 'trained', respectful children. Be careful with toddlers and small ones
With dogs?	Good
With cats?	Usually okay with his 'own'; may chase others
Town or country dog?	Prefers the country
Would he happily live in a flat or apartment?	Yes, with adequate exercise
Natural guard dog?	No
Attitude to strangers?	Friendly

Want to know more?

Breed advice: Glenda Johnson 01570 493221; Margaret McWilliams 01202 715113; Linda Ward 01686 627480
Breed rescue: Mrs Webster 01530 249952

Character sketch

Full of life and mischievous, these are affectionate dogs, who become attached to their family. The breed comes in three styles: Long Haired, Smooth Haired and Wire Haired, and each coat type has two sizes: Miniature and Standard. Wires are outgoing, but Longs are less so; Smooths are middle of the road. It's impossible to venture out with Dachshunds without attracting attention; these instantly recognisable dogs make people smile.

Despite their petite stature and eccentric physique, Dachshunds are tough little characters. These are not small dogs, rather big dogs on short legs.

Special considerations
Keep them from climbing and jumping as young dogs, as they can easily injure their backs. They are prone to putting on weight, so don't overfeed.

History

It has been claimed that a Dachshund-like dog is depicted in Egyptian hieroglyphics, and other theories suggest an ancient Latin American connection. The Dachshund actually emerged in Germany during the 15th century. 'Dachshund' means badger dog, and the breed was used to go to ground after badgers in Germany's dense forests. They were also used to hunt wild boar in packs and they are still commonly used as hunting dogs in many parts of Europe.

One of the first Dachshunds to come to Britain was given as a gift to Queen Victoria by her German relatives in 1845. Animosity towards the Dachshund disappeared after World War I and the breed became more popular than ever during the 1920s in Britain and America.

Like this?
Check out these alternatives:

- Basset Hound
- Cocker Spaniel
- Grand Basset Griffon Vendeen
- Petit Basset Griffon Vendeen

Vital statistics

Height:	Miniatures approx 19-23 cms; Standards approx 30.5-35.5 cms at the shoulder
Weight:	Miniatures 4.5 kgs; Standards 9-12 kgs
Exercise:	●●●○
Grooming:	●●○○
Noise:	●●●○
Food bill:	Around £8 per week

Country of origin:	Germany
Original function:	Hunting
Availability:	Moderate

Colours:	All colours except white
Coat type:	Smooth, Wire or Long
Coat care:	Smooths: a polish with a hound glove; Longs: a daily brush and comb; Wires: stripping twice a year, regular brushing

Health

Average life span:	11½ years
Hereditary disorders:	Eye problems, DNA test for a blood clotting disorder and narcolepsy
Hip dysplasia:	Insufficient numbers have been tested

Suitability

Exercise:	Two half-hour walks a day
Ease of training:	Okay, with patience and motivation
Temperament with children:	Good, though children should be taught to treat the dog respectfully
With dogs?	Okay
With cats?	Okay, if socialised from young. Will probably hunt non-family cats
Town or country dog?	Either
Would he happily live in a flat or apartment?	Not if it involves going up or down stairs
Natural guard dog?	Great watchdogs
Attitude to strangers?	Smooths initially shy; Longs generally laidback; Wires are everyone's friends!

Want to know more?

Breed advice: Anne Moore 01530 271796; Jill Nealis-Vizard 01704 233905; Heather Catterick 01255 677794
Breed rescue: Valerie Skinner 0114 284 7425

History

The first significant evidence of the Dalmatian dates from the middle of the 17th century, with a picture painted by Pieter Boel. The painting depicts a white, smooth-haired dog, covered with black spots, which is not far removed from the dogs we know today.

There is also an old engraving of a spotted dog accompanying an ancient chariot, giving rise to the thought that white, spotted dogs have existed for several thousand years.

It is also believed that once the breed became established in Britain, an amount of Foxhound and Pointer was introduced. Today, they are mostly known as the carriage dogs of the wealthy in Victorian and Edwardian society.

Special considerations

Entire breed has a uric acid problem. Restricted diet and care needed to avoid blockages

Character sketch

The Dalmatian has qualities that point to his ancestry - he has a fine nose and will hunt by scent, he has a soft mouth, and will 'point'. They were bred to be a powerful running dog with amazing stamina - some ran 50 miles with the coach from London to Brighton.

Because of their boundless energy, they are not suitable with very young children, but they are wonderful with older kids and are protective and playful.

The Dalmatian is not the easiest breed to teach. The main thing is to get him to respond to simple commands.

A wonderful companion, devoted and faithful, the Dalmatian is an attractive dog who will command attention wherever he goes.

Like this?
Check out these alternatives:

- Flat Coated Retriever
- German Shorthaired Pointer
- Hungarian Vizsla
- Pointer
- Weimaraner

Vital statistics

Height:	56-61 cms
Weight:	28-32 kgs
Exercise:	●●●●
Grooming:	●○○○
Noise:	●○○○
Food bill:	£8 per week

Country of origin:	Europe-ish
Original function:	General-purpose hunting. Latterly, a carriage dog
Availability:	Easy

Colours:	White with black or liver spots
Coat type:	Smooth and short
Coat care:	Weekly brushing to remove dead hair

Health

Average life span:	12 years
Hereditary disorders:	Deafness and uric acid problem
Hip dysplasia:	11 (breed mean score)

Suitability

Exercise:	This breed needs a lot of exercise, and particularly enjoys free-running
Ease of training:	Reasonable, but patience will reap rewards
Temperament with children:	Very good
With dogs?	Good
With cats?	Okay with his own, take care with others
Town or country dog?	Either
Would he happily live in a flat or apartment?	Not recommended. Must have regular exercise and should never be left alone for long periods
Natural guard dog?	With a little training
Attitude to strangers?	Outgoing

Want to know more?

Breed advice: Shelagh Stevenson 01543 490849; Mr & Mrs Hernandez 01942 236429
Breed rescue: Sue Hemmings 01983 525335

Dandie Dinmont Terrier

History

Breeders of the Dandie see a likeness to both the Bedlington and Border Terriers, but these two breeds are probably only part of the story. Welsh Foxhounds, Otterhounds, Scottish and Bull Terriers have also been suggested as part of the mix! Breeders were originally only concerned with the dogs' capacity and capability for work; with terriers their gameness was of the essence.

The name comes from a character in the novel *Guy Mannering* by Sir Walter Scott, which was published in 1814. Dandie Dinmont had a passion for the hunt and a collection of these odd looking terriers. The Dandie Dinmont Terrier Club was formed in 1875 and a breed standard was created. The standard remains much the same today, and the result is a terrier that breeds true, many of which could still do the job for which they were originally designed. This is still a comparatively rare breed.

Special considerations

Should not be allowed to run up and down stairs or jump on and off furniture, as they can develop back problems. Not good swimmers - take care around unfenced water. It's important to keep them slim, and well-groomed - if neglected, the coat will tangle severely and cause discomfort.

Character sketch

Very self-important, too busy to take much notice of their owner. They are very vocal. They were originally bred to hunt and fight and although these characteristics may be well hidden, potential owners should be aware they will probably surface at some time! He needs plenty of attention and exercise.

Like this?
Check out these alternatives:

- Bedlington Terrier
- Border Terrier
- Dachshund (Wire Haired)
- Petit Basset Griffon Vendeen
- Scottish Terrier

Vital statistics

Height:	20-28 cms
Weight:	8-11 kgs
Exercise:	●●○○
Grooming:	●●●●
Noise:	●●○○
Food bill:	£5 per week

Country of origin:	England
Original function:	Vermin control
Availability:	Difficult

Colours:	Pepper: dark bluish black to silvery grey. Mustard: reddish brown to pale fawn
Coat type:	Harsh top coat growing through thick linty undercoat. Head covered with a profuse silky "top knot"
Coat care:	Daily combing. Professional grooming is recommended three or four times a year

Health

Average life span:	12 years
Hereditary disorders:	Parents and pups should be eye-tested
Hip dysplasia:	Insufficient numbers have been tested

Suitability

Exercise:	As much as you can give, but restricted during the first year to avoid back problems
Ease of training:	Not easy! Patient, kind teaching required
Temperament with children:	Very good
With dogs?	Doesn't pick a fight, but won't back down either - no matter how big the aggressor!
With cats?	Okay with own, watch out with others
Town or country dog?	Country
Would he happily live in a flat or apartment?	Only with understanding of the breed
Natural guard dog?	No, but will warn
Attitude to strangers?	Fine

Want to know more?

Breed advice: Paul Keevil 01342 836240
Breed rescue: Mrs Tinsly 01823 663436

Deerhound

History

Early immigrant sighthounds became the ancestors of several breeds, including the Greyhound and Deerhound.

It's likely that the Irish Wolfhound and the Scottish Deerhound share a common origin, yet the two breeds diverged over the centuries.

By the 1500s, a distinctive, rough-coated sighthound had emerged in the Scottish Highlands. Woodcuts from around 1560 depict Deerhounds pretty much as they are today.

As the 18th century drew to a close, the future was not looking bright for the Deerhound, once known as 'the Royal dog of Scotland'.

But then came the Victorians - who were drawn to the breed, and they enjoyed an upsurge in popularity in the 19th century, which has helped it survive to this day.

Special considerations

The Deerhound should always have something soft to sleep on, as he can suffer pressure sores. He should be kept in lean, hard condition, with plenty of country walks. Be careful if there are pets or livestock in the vicinity.

Character sketch

A quiet, docile dog, the Deerhound is devoted to his family. They are easy to train and eager to please, but they are sensitive.

Care must be taken not to feed an hour either side of exercise to avoid bloat, which can prove fatal. Raising the height of the food bowl helps so that they do not have to reach down to the floor to eat.

Due to their size, Deerhounds are the right height to help themselves from the dinner table or kitchen worktops. You learn to be tidy when you live with a Deerhound!

Like this?
Check out these alternatives:

- Borzoi
- Greyhound
- Irish Wolfhound
- Saluki

Vital statistics

Height:	71-80 cms
Weight:	34-48 kgs
Exercise:	●●○○○
Grooming:	●●○○○
Noise:	●○○○○
Food bill:	£8 per week

Country of origin:	Scotland
Original function:	Hunting deer
Availability:	Not easy

Colours:	Very dark grey to pale grey; some may have red/fawny tinges. Occasionally, a brindle coat will crop up
Coat type:	Shaggy, thick, lying close to the body, crisp to the touch. Must not be woolly
Coat care:	A good brush through once a week

Health

Average life span:	11 years
Hereditary disorders:	DNA test for a blood disorder
Hip dysplasia:	Insufficient numbers have been tested

Suitability

Exercise:	Just puppy play when young. When fully grown, these dogs are inexhaustible and require lots of safe, free-running
Ease of training:	Okay, but they can be choosy about what they want to do!
Temperament with children:	Very good, but make sure that children are equally respectful of the dog
With dogs?	No problems
With cats?	Exercise great caution!
Town or country dog?	Country
Would he happily live in a flat or apartment?	Yes, with adequate exercise; must have access to safe, open spaces
Natural guard dog?	No, but he'll bark at anything unusual
Attitude to strangers?	Aloof initially, while they sum them up

Want to know more?

Breed advice: Elaine Day 01938 559128; Mrs Gudrun Minton 01685 884487
Breed rescue: Sue Reynolds 0121 742 1697

History

Herr Dobermann was a German tax collector, whose job led him to places where thieves lurked. This is quite apart from the farmers who didn't pay their taxes and who were protected by guard dogs. Around 1865, Herr Dobermann began to create a breed that was intelligent, fearless and big enough to tackle dog or man. He started with the advantage that he was an official dog-catcher - in fact, he ran an animal shelter. He had access to many breeds, which makes it difficult to unravel the origin of the Dobermann.

Some experts believe that the basis is the Rottweiler bred to the German Pinscher. Others think he started with mongrels crossed with the Pinscher, producing a bitch that was mated to a Rottweiler type and a sheepdog. There were later infusions of Manchester Terriers, Rottweilers and German Pointers.

Special considerations

Dobermanns like the warmth. He must be trained from a young age with firm kindness. He loves human company, but should be respected. Buy only from reputable breeders who breed for good temperament.

Like this?

Check out these alternatives:

- Manchester Terrier
- Miniature Pinscher
- Pinscher
- Rottweiler
- Standard Smooth Haired Dachshund

Character sketch

An intelligent dog, sensitive to everything that goes on - but the Dobermann is not for everyone. He is very strong, and it is essential for them to be socialised properly from birth.

Unfortunately, some Dobermanns suffer from bloat. A new owner should consult their breeder or vet.

They do like to play, and simple games stimulate their brains, which is necessary for their well-being.

A more loyal and devoted friend does not exist in the canine world than a well-raised Dobermann.

Vital statistics

Height:	65-69 cms
Weight:	29.5-36.5 kgs
Exercise:	●●●○
Grooming:	●○○○
Noise:	●○○○
Food bill:	£8 per week

Country of origin:	Germany
Original function:	Guard dog
Availability:	Easy

Colours:	Black and tan; brown and tan; blue and tan; fawn and tan
Coat type:	Smooth
Coat care:	A weekly brush and polish with a hound glove

Health

Average life span:	10 years
Hereditary disorders:	Eye-test parents and pups, DNA test for blood clotting disorder and narcolepsy
Hip dysplasia:	10 (breed mean score)

Suitability

Exercise:	Lead-walking and free-running twice a day
Ease of training:	Moderate
Temperament with children:	Very good
With dogs?	Males can be difficult with one another
With cats?	Okay with his 'own' cats; generally not good with other cats
Town or country dog?	Country. If a town dog, he should have his own garden
Would he happily live in a flat or apartment?	No, he needs space
Natural guard dog?	Yes
Attitude to strangers?	Suspicious

Want to know more?

Breed advice: Christine Sneddon 01204 880465; Mr & Mrs Bradley 01273 684830
Breed rescue: Sue Garner 01895 253578; Mrs Weston 020 8304 2942; Chris Omar 01276 855326

Dogue De Bordeaux

Dogue De Bordeaux

History

The Dogue De Bordeaux is a member of what can be described as one of the original types of dog, a group called Molossers. They are the breeds from which the Mastiffs in all their variations have evolved. With an absolute certainty giant Mastiff-style dogs have been known for more than 4,000 years.

Much of the history is based on guesswork, so it is impossible to state with certainty how or when the Dogue De Bordeaux evolved into its present type. The assumption must be that they were introduced to Europe by seafaring traders and armies moving up from the Mediterranean area. In the north of Spain and western France, Mastiff dogs were bred with local dogs and slowly as breeds emerged they were called Dogue De Burgos, Dogue De Bordeaux and Dogue d'Acquitaine.

Like this?
Check out these alternatives:

- Boxer
- Bulldog
- Mastiff
- Neapolitan Mastiff
- Rottweiler

Special considerations
Extra care with feeding and exercising of puppies. Needs socialisation and training to control his strength. No exercise or excitement for one hour before feeding and two-three hours after to help prevent bloat.

Character sketch

This is definitely not a dog for a beginner. Although in the family environment they are calm, very affectionate with strong guarding instincts, they are very territorial and do have a stubborn nature.

For someone who is prepared to give the Dogue De Bordeaux the training he needs, the amount of food with the correct exercise and above all the space he needs will have an intelligent companion, whose sole interest will be to be with and to serve his human family.

Vital statistics

Height:	58-68 cms
Weight:	At least 45-50 kgs
Exercise:	●●●●
Grooming:	●●○○
Noise:	●●●○
Food bill:	£10 a week

Country of origin:	France
Original function:	Guard
Availability:	Difficult

Colours:	Tawny or any shade of fawn, small amount of white on feet and chest acceptable. Red or black mask
Coat type:	Fine, short and soft to touch
Coat care:	Weekly brushing

Health

Average life span:	11 years
Hereditary disorders:	Eye-test parents, DNA test for blood clotting disorder
Hip dysplasia:	23 (breed mean score)

Suitability

Exercise:	Daily substantial walks and garden play
Ease of training:	Start young with kind, patient training, can be stubborn
Temperament with children:	Good but don't leave alone with toddlers, can be clumsy
With dogs?	Take care with all breeds, some are dominant
With cats?	Take care
Town or country dog?	Country
Would he happily live in a flat or apartment?	Not really suitable
Natural guard dog?	Yes
Attitude to strangers?	Suspicious

Want to know more?

Breed advice: Adrian Bicknell 01342 842705
Breed rescue: Carol Cavanagh 01342 842705

History

Springer Spaniels are as English as a cup of tea. And yet, just like the nation's favourite beverage, the English Springer Spaniel is not indigenous to these shores. Although their precise origin is hazy, it's likely that spaniels arrived in this country from Spain, probably via France, at the time of the reign of Queen Elizabeth I.

The earliest English reference to spaniels is found in a book, *Master of Game,* which was written in 1406. Spaniels were used to flush, or 'spring', game birds towards a hawk or net. Later, hunting with guns became popular and spaniels were used to startle birds into flying into the line of fire.

Like this?
Check out these alternatives:

- Brittany
- Cocker Spaniel
- Field Spaniel
- Irish Red and White Setter
- Welsh Springer Spaniel

Character sketch

The Springer is a super family dog. From a very young age a puppy will be looking for things to do, particularly things to carry. It is difficult to train them out of this habit, as they are genetically programmed to retrieve.

By nature they are mega-energetic, especially when young, and they need to be kept at the peak of fitness with frequent exercise. Ideally, part of the day should be set aside for games; this exercises them and helps to stimulate their brains, which is needed because they are very intelligent.

The English Springer Spaniel is affable and gentle. Training is important, because of the breed's energetic nature, but your dog will repay the effort a thousand times over.

Special considerations
The English Springer is bouncy and can be boisterous, so start training from puppyhood. Be careful with food - the breed is prone to obesity.

Vital statistics

Height:	51 cms (the 'working' type is generally smaller overall)
Weight:	20.5-23 kgs
Exercise:	●●●●
Grooming:	●●●○
Noise:	●●○○
Food bill:	£9 per week

Country of origin:	Britain
Original function:	Springing game
Availability:	Moderate

Colours:	Liver and white; black and white
Coat type:	Straight, not coarse, with moderate feathering
Coat care:	Thorough weekly groom, with feathering combed through after every walk

Health

Average life span:	14 years
Hereditary disorders:	Eye-test parents and pups and DNA test for metabolic disorders
Hip dysplasia:	14 (breed mean score)

Suitability

Exercise:	A good walk twice a day (minimum of half-hour each) for adult dogs; with free-running and plenty of quality play
Ease of training:	Responds well to reward-based methods
Temperament with children:	Excellent
With dogs?	No problems
With cats?	Okay, if brought up with them
Town or country dog?	Either, though he prefers country life
Would he happily live in a flat or apartment?	Only if there is access to a safe garden and the dog is given adequate exercise
Natural guard dog?	No, but will warn if strangers approach
Attitude to strangers?	Friendly with strangers

Want to know more?

Breed advice: Christine Winfield 01858 575721
Breed rescue: Selina Clarke 01752 691579

History

Many types of terrier were once bred in the Lake District. These dogs were highly localised and sometimes varied from village to village. For working trial purposes, this mixture of terriers was often known generically as Fell Terriers or Lakeland Terriers. The Patterdale - a black Fell Terrier - is a popular dog, and many people are not aware that the Fell Terrier exists at all - let alone in other colours. The village of Patterdale, in Cumbria, is not actually the home of this feisty terrier. Indeed, Cyril Breay, who helped develop the breed in the 1950s, was reportedly miffed when the name 'Patterdale' became attached to his favourite breed. The Cumbrian fells are still very much a working agricultural landscape. Foxes were, and still are, regarded by many Lakeland farmers as a pest. Consequently, Lake District terriers were bred to kill a fox outright.

Character sketch

Like a wound-up spring, this dog is never still. Tough and cheeky, he'll find mischief even if it's not there! An escape-proof garden is a must, as these canine Houdinis can slip through gaps and climb wire-mesh fences.

The Fell Terrier should not be let off the lead on walks, no matter how well trained, as he will find it difficult to restrain himself if a furry animal comes into sight.

A naturally affectionate dog, the Fell Terrier wants be part of everything the family does.

Like this?
Check out these alternatives:

- Border Terrier
- Irish Terrier
- Lakeland Terrier
- Norfolk Terrier
- Parson Russell Terrier

Special considerations
Do not feed a high-protein diet unless the dog is working hard. Fell Terriers must be exercised properly or they will get tetchy.

Vital statistics

Height:	30.5-33 cms
Weight:	5.5-8 kgs
Exercise:	●●●●
Grooming:	●●○○
Noise:	●●○○
Food bill:	£8 per week

Country of origin:	Britain's north country
Original function:	Vermin control
Availability:	Moderate

Colours:	Black, red, black and tan, wheaten, blue, chocolate
Coat type:	Three coat types: wire, rough or smooth
Coat care:	A quick comb through once or twice a week. The rough or wire coat should be handstripped once or twice a year

Health

Average life span:	15 years
Hereditary disorders:	No problems known to breeders
Hip dysplasia:	Insufficient numbers have been tested

Suitability

Exercise:	Needs all you can give - and more!
Ease of training:	Not easy, though the breed is intelligent. Patience required
Temperament with children:	Very good if respected
With dogs?	Bit iffy; dogs in particular can be argumentative
With cats?	Okay if socialised with a family cat as a puppy, but other cats are a big no no!
Town or country dog?	Country
Would he happily live in a flat or apartment?	No
Natural guard dog?	A good watchdog
Attitude to strangers?	Suspicious

Want to know more?

Breed advice: Juliet Shaw 01233 720340
Breed rescue: No known rescue

Special considerations
Hates to be left alone. Needs to be trained from young. For the best results, teach him with patience and kindness.

History

Initially, dogs were called retrievers because of what they did rather than what they were, and breeds as diverse as Scottish Terriers, Deerhounds, Bloodhounds and terrier-Bulldog crosses were all variously described as retrievers by commentators on dog matters in the 19th century.

The ever-popular Labrador Retriever arrived in Britain in the early 1800s aboard fishing boats from the Canadian province of Newfoundland. His skill, both on land and in water, was quickly recognised and the breed was crossed with Water Spaniels and Poodles to give us the Curly Coated Retriever, and with setters to produce the Flat Coated Retriever, which was originally known as the Wavy Coat.

In 1878, JH Walsh, then editor of *The Field,* concluded that the Flat Coated Retriever had evolved into a specific breed: "Whilst all kinds of dogs were Retrievers, the world of 1877 demanded a Retriever proper, black by preference, and either wavy-coated or curly."

Character sketch

This is a very affectionate dog with a warped sense of humour. He is one of the most gentle, happy and loving breeds in the world. Also, the Flat Coat requires things to do - he needs to be stimulated both in mind and in body.

Properly fed and exercised, the Flat Coated Retriever will remain active right into old age.

Living in the country with an active family, the Flat Coat will prove himself to be the most amiable of dogs.

Like this?
Check out these alternatives:

- English Setter
- Golden Retriever
- Labrador Retriever
- Large Munsterlander

Vital statistics

Height:	58-61 cms
Weight:	25 36 kgs
Exercise:	●●●●
Grooming:	●●●○
Noise:	●○○○
Food bill:	£7 per week

Country of origin:	England
Original function:	Retrieving
Availability:	Difficult

Colours:	Black or liver
Coat type:	A weatherproof undercoat, and a medium-length topcoat. The texture should not be silky or harsh
Coat care:	Twice-weekly brush and comb; daily grooming needed when moulting

Health

Average life span:	10 years
Hereditary disorders:	Eye-test parents and pups
Hip dysplasia:	9 (breed mean score)

Suitability

Exercise:	They'll take as much as you can give; allow a short rest afterwards and then do it all again!
Ease of training:	Learn quickly, but will forget as easily!
Temperament with children:	Very good, but they can be 'licky'. Tails can be a problem with toddlers around
With dogs?	Reasonably okay
With cats?	Good with his 'own'; very bad with others
Town or country dog?	Prefers the country
Would he happily live in a flat or apartment?	Not really
Natural guard dog?	No, but will give a warning bark
Attitude to strangers?	Almost too friendly!

Want to know more?

 Breed advice: Denise Jury 01246 856791 or 07734 233731
Breed rescue: Mary Haines 01666 837087; Evelin Lee 01772 614715

German Shepherd Dog

History

Archaeological digs in northern Holland and Turkestan provide proof that this type of dog existed in the Bronze Age - skeletal remains have been found of a very similar type of dog, together with those of sheep. The Roman historian Tacitus wrote of the "wolf-like dogs of the country around the Rhine". From the mid 19th century, enthusiasts started to breed to a particular standard and type, and in 1901 the Verein für Deutsche Schäferhunde (Club for German Shepherd Dogs) was formed. Known as the SV, this club sought to produce the ultimate shepherd's dog - intelligent, strong, agile and hardy, with a weatherproof coat. The SV still has a profound influence on the GSD today.

The breed first came to the attention of the British during the First World War, when they were used by the Germans to locate the wounded, and to carry supplies. Captured dogs were brought back by returning British soldiers and renamed 'Alsatians'. Today, the German Shepherd Dog is the most popular breed of dog in the world.

Character sketch

The German Shepherd is a loyal and devoted guardian - an easily-trained, affectionate dog who will enhance the life of any family. In their service to humans, GSDs have no equal - rescue dogs, sniffer dogs, tracking dogs, Customs and Excise dogs, assistance dogs - the German Shepherd can turn its paw to anything.

Like this?
Check out these alternatives:

- Akita
- Alaskan Malamute
- Belgian Shepherd Dog (all types)

Special considerations
The German Shepherd needs contact with humans, but should receive kind, firm training. For both his physical and mental stability, he must have plenty of exercise and things to keep him occupied.

Vital statistics

Height:	58-63 cms
Weight:	Varies according to the type of dog
Exercise:	●●●●●
Grooming:	●●●●
Noise:	●●●●
Food bill:	£10 per week

Country of origin:	Germany
Original function:	Herding and livestock security
Availability:	Easy

Colours:	All colours, but whites, blues and livers are not desired by the show world
Coat type:	Show type: harsh outercoat and a thick undercoat. Long-haired type: undercoat covered with a long, soft overcoat
Coat care:	Weekly brush and comb

Health

Average life span:	10$^{1}/_{2}$ years
Hereditary disorders:	Parents and pups should be eye-tested. Males should be tested for haemophilia before breeding. DNA tests available.
Hip dysplasia:	19 (breed mean score)

Suitability

Exercise:	Lots of exercise, to include free-running and controlled walking
Ease of training:	With their high intelligence, very easy
Temperament with children:	Excellent
With dogs?	Okay
With cats?	Good with own; with others - watch it!
Town or country dog?	Country
Would he happily live in a flat or apartment?	Only if exercised frequently
Natural guard dog?	Yes
Attitude to strangers?	Suspicious

Want to know more?

Breed advice: Sandra Redpath 01724 783797; Lesley Keeley 01424 814548; Gail Gwesyn-Pryce 01686 688920

Breed rescue: Geoff and Val Pardy 01923 852452

Character sketch

A happy-go-lucky dog who tends to favour one person in the household. Independent and intelligent, they aren't usually lapdogs. Many have a penchant for playing in water.

Special considerations

Watch your dog's weight as he gets older. With the Klein variety, remember to treat him like a dog and not a toy!

Like this?

Check out these alternatives:

- Pomeranian
- Japanese Spitz
- Samoyed

History

The history of the German Spitz isn't as easy to pin down as you might think. Germany didn't actually exist until 1871, but the ancestors of these dogs were running around northern Europe in the Neolithic age - remains have been found in peat bogs. It's possible that the spitz breeds originally came from the Arctic and are related to Samoyeds, Huskies and other such breeds. How they travelled south, though, we can only speculate - it's possible they were transported by Vikings. The trail gets a bit muddy after this though. They continued to be used as sled, cart and guard dogs, and their coats were shorn and woven into cloth. Slowly, they also became companion dogs, and smaller versions became popular.

Queen Charlotte imported some spitz dogs from Germany in the 1760s. They also found favour with the painter Thomas Gainsborough, who painted *Pomeranian with her Puppy* in 1771. The term "Pomeranian" appears to have been used as a generic term for all these unusual spitz breeds. It was actually Queen Victoria who introduced the miniature versions into this country. The German Spitz was recognised by the Kennel Club in 1985.

Vital statistics

Height:	Klein 23-29 cms; Mittel 30-38 cms
Weight:	Klein around 5 kgs; Mittel 10 kgs
Exercise:	●●○○
Grooming:	●●●○
Noise:	●●●●
Food bill:	£8 per week

Country of origin:	Germany
Original function:	Watchdog
Availability:	Difficult

Colours:	Every colour and marking combination possible
Coat type:	A soft, woolly undercoat, covered in a straight harsh-textured topcoat
Coat care:	A brush and comb through twice a week

Health

Average life span:	14 years
Hereditary disorders:	None known to breeders
Hip dysplasia:	Insufficient numbers have been tested

Suitability

Exercise:	Will be happy with two half-hour exercise periods a day, but will take more
Ease of training:	Reasonably easy
Temperament with children:	Good, provided they are treated with respect
With dogs? Good	
With cats?	Okay with own if properly socialised and introduced; take care with others
Town or country dog?	Either
Would he happily live in a flat or apartment?	Yes
Natural guard dog?	No, but a good watchdog
Attitude to strangers?	Initially suspicious

Want to know more?

Breed advice: Chris King 0121 706 6944; Helen Banfield 01753 735778

Breed rescue: Mrs H Gillies 01406 330056

German Wirehaired Pointer

History

These hunting dogs probably originated in southern Europe, where a variety of hunting dogs emerged around the 17th century. Originally, hunters used nets to catch game birds, so they needed a dog that would detect and then 'freeze' a bird for long enough for the huntsmen to throw the net.

This practice gives the pointer its distinctive pose: with head held high and one leg raised - as if it is literally pointing at its prey. Later, guns were used, but early firearms were slow to load and dogs were still a useful tool to 'hold' the game.

Germany has several rough-coated pointers (as well as long- and short-haired varieties) and the German Wirehaired Pointer, like its cousins, is the result of a lot of mixing and matching. Depending on which sources you go to, the GWP's ancestors include Poodles, Airedale Terriers, Foxhounds, French Griffons as well as any or all of the other German pointing breeds.

Like this?
Check out these alternatives:

- German Shorthaired Pointer
- Giant Schnauzer
- Hungarian Wirehaired Vizsla
- Italian Spinone
- Slovakian Roughhaired Pointer

Special considerations
If bored and left to his own devices, this dog can trash a home in minutes! The GWP needs mental and physical stimulation - and company.

Character sketch

An eager gundog, with a keen nose, the German Wirehaired Pointer is happy to work in water or on land. Alert and energetic, he makes a trustworthy companion. Also, they are gentle, affectionate and even-tempered.

Show or working, the GWP is a dual-purpose gundog that combines beauty with brains. Adults of the breed have unlimited energy, relish exercise, and will take as much working and free-running as you can give. They also love swimming.

Vital statistics

Height:	56-67 cms
Weight:	20.5-34 kgs
Exercise:	●●●●
Grooming:	●●○○
Noise:	●●○○
Food bill:	£8 a week

Country of origin:	Germany
Original function:	Hunt, point and retrieve
Availability:	Not easy

Colours:	Liver; liver and white; black and white
Coat type:	Thick and harsh with thick undercoat, bushy eyebrows and beard
Coat care:	A thorough brush once a week. Twice a year, the coat needs to be handstripped

Health

Average life span:	13 years
Hereditary disorders:	DNA test for a blood clotting condition
Hip dysplasia:	11 (breed mean score)

Suitability

Exercise:	Adaptable, but requires daily exercise - ideally free-running
Ease of training:	Generally amenable, though some have a stubborn streak. Needs firm boundaries
Temperament with children:	Generally good; children, of course, must be respectful in return
With dogs?	No problems, with early socialisation
With cats?	Friendly if raised and socialised with them from puppyhood
Town or country dog?	Prefers country life, but is adaptable
Would he happily live in a flat or apartment?	With company, but he prefers to live with his human family
Natural guard dog?	No, but he will warn if strangers knock
Attitude to strangers?	Aloof

Want to know more?

Breed advice: Maxine McCullough 01744 633724
Breed rescue: Sharon Pinkerton 01536 770714

Character sketch

Fairly active, they are the most versatile of all dogs and one of the greatest companions.

It takes little time for a Golden puppy to discover that he can please his doting owner by carrying a slipper or a newspaper, and, from that, it is a simple task to teach him to bring any object within his strength.

The Golden Retriever is intelligent, and will learn many tricks and understand a wide vocabulary if given enough stimulation.

He has a penchant for swimming - a run by a stretch of water is his idea of heaven.

History

Mrs Charlesworth, the founder of the Golden Retriever Club, wrote that, in 1856, Sir Marjoribanks, later to be Lord Tweedmouth, saw a Russian troupe of performing dogs (sheepdog/retriever types) in a circus in Brighton. He became so enamoured that he bought eight of them. Over the following 20 years, the breed began losing its mental alertness, stamina, and working capability. His Lordship sent his agent to Russia to find fresh blood, but failed to track down a single specimen - it was rumoured that the breed existed in the more remote areas of Asiatic Russia.

In the mid 1800s, there were several breeds of water dogs; it was from the union of a yellow Tweed Water Spaniel called Belle, with Nous, a yellowish, wavy- or flat-coated retriever of indeterminate origin, that the Goldie stems.

Like this?
Check out these alternatives:

- Flat Coated Retriever
- Labrador Retriever
- Pyrenean Mountain Dog

Special considerations
Buy only from a responsible breeder, make sure you see test results (BVA/ KC schemes of parents), and see the puppy with his mother.

Vital statistics

Height:	51-61 cms
Weight:	Around 32kg
Exercise:	●●●○
Grooming:	●●●○
Noise:	●●○○
Food bill:	£8 a week

Country of origin:	Scotland
Original function:	Retrieving game
Availability:	Easy

Colours:	Pale cream to rich gold - not mahogany or Irish Setter red!
Coat type:	Long guard hairs, with a soft undercoat
Coat care:	Weekly brush and comb

Health

Average life span:	13 years
Hereditary disorders:	Eye-test parents and pups and DNA test for muscular dystrophy
Hip dysplasia:	18 (breed mean score)

Suitability

Exercise:	Adores exercise, but will be content with two walks daily
Ease of training:	Easy
Temperament with children:	Really good
With dogs?	Okay
With cats?	Okay with own, but take care with others!
Town or country dog?	Both, but prefers country
Would he happily live in a flat or apartment?	Wouldn't be happy in a flat, but could adapt to a kennel if he had company
Natural guard dog?	No
Attitude to strangers?	Friendly

Want to know more?

Breed advice: Mary Potter 01386 438040; Mark Spring 01406 422407; Kim Ellis 01980 653109
Breed rescue: Mrs Robinson 01257 262416; Laurina Blankenspoor 0845 166 2072

Gordon Setter

History

Black and tan setters have been around for a very long time, oil paintings from 1600 prove the point, at that time they were described as a 'Black and Fallow Setting dog'. The Gordon Setter was popular among the aristocrats and monied classes in the middle to late 19th century. Without doubt their absolute origin lies in the early spaniels, which are said to come from Spain.

Over the years, by a process of selective breeding, their shape and working inclination has been changed. Their long legs allow them to see and smell game birds in long grass and ferns and in the middle of the 1800s they were among the most popular of gundogs.

Character sketch

A great companion dog if trained with firm kindness. Intelligent and bold of character, he will act on his own initiative. They are a most agreeable dog to have around either as a working gundog or a house pet. They are gentle and caring towards their human family, sometimes attaching themselves to a single person.

It has to be remembered that this breed is a working breed: they need to be out and about, they need exercise - as much as possible to stimulate their bodies and minds. They can be easily trained.

The Gordon Setter would grace any country house and bring pleasure to each member of the family.

English Setters

All the setters had a similar job. The English Setter is said to be the oldest, being developed 400 years ago. Of all the setter breeds, the English is probably the most suitable for family life.

Special considerations

Care must be taken not to overfeed Gordon Setters when young and caution with additives is needed. Youngsters should not have too much exercise, at least until they are about nine months of age. Build strength slowly.

Like this?
Check out these alternatives:

- English Setter
- English Springer Spaniel
- Irish Red and White Setter
- Irish Setter
- Large Munsterlander

Vital statistics

Height:	62-66 cms
Weight:	25.5-29.5 kgs
Exercise:	●●●●
Grooming:	●●●○
Noise:	●●○○
Food bill:	£7 a week

Country of origin:	Scotland
Original function:	Bird dog
Availability:	Difficult

Colours:	Black with lustrous tan markings on head. Two tan spots on chest and legs
Coat type:	Moderate length, free of wave and curl, legs, ears and belly feathered
Coat care:	Regular brushing on body and combing of feathering

Health

Average life span:	13 years
Hereditary disorders:	Heart problems
Hip dysplasia:	23 (breed mean score)

Suitability

Exercise:	This is a running outside dog and needs plenty of exercise to maintain physical and mental health
Ease of training:	Easy, very biddable
Temperament with children:	Really good but needs respect
With dogs?	Basically friendly, some dominance with own breed
With cats?	Good with own, be careful with others
Town or country dog?	Country
Would he happily live in a flat or apartment?	No
Natural guard dog?	Very alert, will give warning
Attitude to strangers?	Cautious

Want to know more?

 Breed advice & rescue: Jill Dixon 01260 290676

History

Engravings of Danish hunting scenes from the 1860s depict Great Danes. It's likely that the breed had also found its way to Britain by the 1800s, and something closely resembling the Great Dane was once called the *English Dogge*. Whatever you want to call them, early editions of these noble giants were hunting boar during the Middle Ages.

The Great Dane was not short of gainful employment. There is evidence that the dogs carried lanterns for travellers who welcomed the protection. They also pulled carts and joined forces with Dalmatians to work as carriage dogs. They were initially recruited as security personnel, but these mighty, impressive-looking dogs soon became a fashion must-have for any well-turned-out retinue.

Character sketch

A protective breed, he sounds fierce but is never aggressive. One of the most endearing traits of the Dane's character is his fondness for his family.

Dane puppies grow quickly and it is important to regulate the growth rate with the right food and the correct protein level. Exercise must also be controlled.

With generous TLC, and correct feeding and exercise, your puppy will, no doubt, grow into a fine family pet, one who will fill your life with endless pleasure.

Special considerations
Needs soft bedding or he can suffer from calluses on the elbows. His food bowl should be two feet off the ground. Exercise him in the morning before feeding, and give one hour's rest afterwards. A light lunch, with the main food in the evening is ideal. Strictly no exercise for one hour after food.

Like this?
Check out these alternatives:

- Anatolian Shepherd Dog
- Deerhound
- Hamiltonstövare
- Hungarian Vizsla

Vital statistics

Height:	71-76 cms
Weight:	46-54 kgs
Exercise:	●●○○
Grooming:	●○○○
Noise:	●●○○
Food bill:	£11 a week

Country of origin:	Germany
Original function:	Hunting boar
Availability:	Moderate

Colours:	Brindle, fawn, blue, black, harlequin (white with black or blue patches on top). White permissible on the chest and feet
Coat type:	Short, dense and sleek
Coat care:	Weekly brushing with a firm brush, finishing with a hound glove

Health

Average life span:	8 years
Hereditary disorders:	Deafness, eye-test parents and pups
Hip dysplasia:	13 (breed mean score)

Suitability

Exercise:	Two 20-minute walks a day
Ease of training:	Gentle, firm and consistent training is needed
Temperament with children:	Excellent, provided he's been well socialised with them
With dogs?	Good, provided he's been well socialised
With cats?	Ditto
Town or country dog?	Flexible, but he needs things to do, especially if he's living in a town
Would he happily live in a flat or apartment?	Yes, with sufficient mental and physical stimulation
Natural guard dog?	Yes, in size - but not in temperament
Attitude to strangers?	Aloof. Does not allow over-familiarity

Want to know more?

Breed advice: Sue Satterley 01460 52676
Breed rescue: Liz and Gordon Davies 01267 290317; Helen Evans 01792 424401

Greyhound

Special considerations
In very cold weather, keep them warm. They must be allowed to run freely (in a safe, enclosed area).

Like this?
Check out these alternatives:

- Borzoi
- Deerhound
- Italian Greyhound
- Saluki
- Whippet

History

It seems likely that there were Greyhounds in Britain as early as the 800s. They were probably brought to western Europe by Celts migrating from the east. By this time, sighthounds already had a long and distinguished pedigree across Persia, Greece, Rome and the Arab world. For much of the last thousand years, no royal retinue was complete without Greyhounds. Virtually every king, queen, prince, lord, duke or earl in Europe kept Greyhounds, and these dogs are a common feature of royal portraiture. In recent times, Greyhounds have lost their regal reputation and become instead associated with a sporting life.

Each year, 10,000 Greyhounds retire from the track, and finally people are starting to take notice of their plight. Over the past few years, animal charities and concerned individuals have been working tirelessly to rescue and rehome Greyhounds, and to restore their reputation as worthy companions.

Character sketch

This is a gentle, affectionate dog, who likes nothing more than to be with his family. They have a quiet nature - come home after a couple of hours' shopping and a little wave of the tail, a lick on the hand and an adoring look will melt your heart.

They are sprinters by nature (a typical race lasts 30 seconds), but they are quite content with a couple of 20-minute walks a day, and this can be on-lead walking.

They are also calm and laid-back - ideal companions!

Vital statistics

Height:	69-76 cms
Weight:	30-40 kgs
Exercise:	●●○○
Grooming:	●○○○
Noise:	●○○○
Food bill:	£8 per week

Country of origin:	Egypt
Original function:	Hunting
Availability:	Easy

Colours:	Black, white, red, blue, fawn, fallow, brindle, or any of these colours broken with white
Coat type:	Flat, short and smooth
Coat care:	A weekly brush to remove dead hair is all that is needed

Health

Average life span:	12 years
Hereditary disorders:	No problems known to breeders
Hip dysplasia:	Insufficient numbers have been tested

Suitability

Exercise:	Couch potatoes who love a good, short, sharp sprint (in a safe location) plus two 20-minute on-lead walks a day
Ease of training:	Moderate
Temperament with children:	Very good
With dogs?	No problems
With cats?	Many happily live with cats after careful introductions, but caution must be taken
Town or country dog?	Either, but prefers the country
Would he happily live in a flat or apartment?	Yes, if taken out regularly
Natural guard dog?	Not really
Attitude to strangers?	Fine

Want to know more?

Breed advice: Jeffery Burrell 01933 381089 **Breed rescue:** The Greyhound Trust 0161 223 8000; The Retired Greyhound Trust 0870 4440673; Greyhound Welfare South Wales & West (Paula Ambrose) 01633 892846

Character sketch

Happy and adventurous, the Griffon Bruxellois adores his family and always wants to be included in activities.

The Griffon's twinkling eyes betray one of his endearing traits: mischief. They are fun dogs, full of little quirks to amuse their owners.

There is a scarcity of these dogs, but if you are lucky enough to find one, you will have a joyous companion for a long time. The breed suits everyone. For the older owner, Griffons are easily handled; they also suit the young, as they are full of life.

Like this?
Check out these alternatives:

- Affenpinscher
- Border Terrier
- Miniature Schnauzer
- Norfolk Terrier

History

Small but hardy rough-coated dogs were known across Belgium from at least the Middle Ages. These tenacious dogs were kept as farmyard ratters, but they were also a popular subject matter for artists. Pierre-Auguste Renoir's 1870 portrait, *La Baigneuse au Griffon* (Bather with a Griffon), depicts a dog that clearly has more than one or two genes in common with our contemporary canine.

The modern Griffon Bruxellois is more than likely the result of a deliberate concoction that was produced in Brussels in the late 1800s. It's thought that Affenpinschers were crossed with toy dogs, such as Pugs and Ruby Spaniels, to create a working dog suited to city life. Their scruffy appearance earned them the nickname 'Belgian street urchin'.

Griffons became popular across Belgian society and received a considerable boost when Queen Henrietta Maria took a shine to the breed in the 1870s.

Special considerations
Treat the Griffon Bruxellois like a normal dog with plenty of TLC. Just because he's small, does not make him a play thing.

Vital statistics

Height:	27-28 cms
Weight:	2.7-4.5 kgs
Exercise:	●●○○
Grooming:	●●●○
Noise:	●●●○
Food bill:	£5 per week

Country of origin:	Belgium
Original function:	Ratter for stables
Availability:	Difficult

Colours:	Black, red, black and tan
Coat type:	Harsh and wiry, with an undercoat
Coat care:	A brush and comb through twice a week. The coat needs to be stripped every three months

Health

Average life span:	14 years
Hereditary disorders:	Eye test parents
Hip dysplasia:	Insufficient numbers have been tested

Suitability

Exercise:	Two 20-minute walks a day, plus play in the garden, though he will take more
Ease of training:	Easy - generally co-operative
Temperament with children:	Good, provided he's treated with respect
With dogs?	Usually okay, though some males can be rather dominant with others
With cats?	Generally okay with his 'own'; with other cats, exercise caution
Town or country dog?	Either
Would he happily live in a flat or apartment?	Yes, if provided with adequate exercise
Natural guard dog?	Will warn you of anything unusual
Attitude to strangers?	Some are suspicious, some are friendly

Want to know more?

Breed advice: Betty Gorringe 01202 891820
Breed rescue: Betty Gorringe 01202 891820; Mrs M Higgins 01977 558363

History

The Hamiltonstövare is a unique dog, originally bred by the Swedes. They wanted a tough hound, capable of working by himself in the bitter cold of northern Sweden.

How this was achieved is obscure, but there are several theories. One is that the Hamiltonstövare is a mixture of eastern European hounds brought to Sweden in the 15th and 16th centuries with Swiss Hounds and Foxhounds. Another is that the Hanover Hound, the Holstein Hound, the Latvian Curland Hound and the Foxhound form the basis of the breed. Lastly, the Hamiltonstövare could be a straight cross between the Hanover Hound and the Foxhound.

Whatever the origins of the breed, the end product is unique, in as much as they hunt singly. They were not bred to kill; they drive the game, giving voice while on the scent.

Character sketch

A calm, affectionate breed, Hamiltons are a joy to live with. They are not a dog for just anyone, however; they need a very energetic and patient owner. They dislike being left alone for hours and do not know the difference between Chippendale and MFI furniture - it'll get chewed just the same when they are bored, and, without action, they bore easily.

This is a dog for the active family that has plenty of room and an understanding of the needs of this dynamic breed.

Special considerations
He should be kept on a lead in public places because he may be some time before coming back! Exercise and companionship are of prime importance - for both his physical and mental health.

Like this?
Check out these alternatives:

- Beagle
- Bernese Mountain Dog
- Bloodhound
- Dalmatian
- Labrador Retriever

Vital statistics

Height:	43-61 cms
Weight:	25-35 kgs
Exercise:	●●●●
Grooming:	●○○○
Noise:	●●●●
Food bill:	About £8 a week

Country of origin:	Sweden
Original function:	Solo hunter
Availability:	Difficult

Colours:	Tri-colour (black, deep tan and white)
Coat type:	Soft, thick undercoat, covered with a harsh, weather-resistant top-coat
Coat care:	Weekly brush and comb, more when he moults twice a year

Health

Average life span:	11½ years
Hereditary disorders:	No problems known to breeders
Hip dysplasia:	Insufficient numbers have been tested

Suitability

Exercise:	One hour of on-lead road-walking daily, plus a secure garden to free run
Ease of training:	Not easy
Temperament with children:	Really excellent
With dogs?	Very good
With cats?	Okay with his own cats
Town or country dog?	Country preferred, but, given enough exercise, he will happily adapt to town life
Would he happily live in a flat or apartment?	Only with sufficient exercise
Natural guard dog?	No
Attitude to strangers?	Not suspicious

Want to know more?

Breed advice & rescue: Diane Cook 01420 86183

History

From Roman times Pliny the Elder (AD 23-79) mentioned a breed that fits the description of the Havanese in his encyclopaedia *Historia Naturalis*.

Other authorities seek to prove that the origin is in ancient Egypt, yet another theorises the breed was bought back from India by Alexander the Great.

What is almost certain is that one prime ancestor is the Barbet, an ancient Mediterranean Water Spaniel who exists to this day.

Havanese enthusiasts claim the country of origin to be Cuba, but how did they get there if their true origin is around the Mediterranean? Christopher Columbus discovered Cuba in 1492 and the Spanish colonised it from 1511. After the menfolk had settled, what was more natural than to send for their wives who would bring their pets?

During the latter part of the 19th century owning a Havanese was high fashion among the society ladies in Cuba and the USA.

Special considerations
Lack of human company distresses them; they hate being alone.

Like this?
Check out these alternatives:

- Bichon Frise
- Bolognese
- Maltese
- Shih Tzu
- Tibetan Terrier

Character sketch

The Havanese is a dependable, faithful dog. He is a gentle, responsive and sometimes shy companion.

This breed is much calmer than its cousin, the Bichon Frise, preferring a quieter life. Although they are still playful, they are not boisterous. They are not a yappy dog by nature although other breeds can train them to be noisy.

One of the outstanding characteristics is their total devotion to their owners, they become a veritable shadow. They must be treated kindly, and they are easily upset if the owner is angry.

Vital statistics

Height:	23-28 cms
Weight:	Ideally 4.5-5.5 kgs
Exercise:	●○○○
Grooming:	●●●●
Noise:	●●○○
Food bill:	£5 a week

Country of origin:	Cuba
Original function:	Companion
Availability:	Very difficult

Colours:	All colours permissible
Coat type:	Long and silky with a light curl - full coat with undercoat
Coat care:	If neglected, the coat mats and tangles badly

Health

Average life span:	14 years
Hereditary disorders:	Eye-test parents
Hip dysplasia:	Insufficient numbers have been tested

Suitability

Exercise:	An hour a day is sufficient - and they love playing in the garden too
Ease of training:	Moderate
Temperament with children	Very tolerant, but children must be taught how to handle them gently as they can be shy
With dogs?	Good
With cats?	Okay with 'own', but take care around others
Town or country dog?	Either
Would he happily live in a flat or apartment?	Yes
Natural guard dog?	Will bark a short warning
Attitude to strangers?	Slightly suspicious

Want to know more?

Breed advice: Jill Richards 01773 716021; Wendy Allenby 01472 821758
Breed rescue: Linda Kidger 01472 591358

History

During the eighth and ninth centuries nomadic tribes such as the Magyars and the Huns travelled west from Asia in huge caravans, bringing with them their horses, cattle and sheep - the Great Migration. Of course, they brought their dogs too, to drive and protect the livestock. The Magyars settled on the spacious plains of Hungary. They cared little how their dogs looked, as long as they could work in temperatures over 40°C at the height of summer, and -20° in the depths of winter. A good dog was a valuable asset; if he failed to perform, he would be killed and replaced without compassion. Over time, breeds were created that could survive on small amounts of food, were enthusiastic, fearless, hardy and intelligent. The Puli is still used as a working sheepdog today.

Like this?
Check out these alternatives:
- Löwchen
- Tibetan Terrier
- Komondor

Character sketch

Very active and highly intelligent, this breed is best described as a country dog, although, with enough exercise, he will adapt to town life.

Special considerations
The mark of the Puli is its coat, trailing to the ground in long cords. There are different types of coat: the naturally corded and a matted, felted coat; unfortunately, this type of coat has to have frequent attention. It is possible to cut the coat of a pet dog and keep it at about two inches long; combing it regularly will stop cording or matting. If it is naturally corded, keep the cords about four inches long. The show-goer must be prepared for work, at least until the dog is about 18 months old when the coat finishes development. Cords must be separated and not allowed to felt.

Vital statistics

Height:	37-44 cms
Weight:	10-15 kgs
Exercise:	●●○○
Grooming:	●●●●
Noise:	●●○○
Food bill:	£7.50 per week

Country of origin:	Hungary
Original function:	Sheep herder and stock guard
Availability:	Difficult

Colours:	Black, rusty black, white, shades of grey
Coat type:	Two types of coat, thick cords and thin cords. The correct proportion between top and undercoat creates the cords. Matting and felting to be avoided
Coat care:	See 'Special Considerations' box

Health

Average life span:	11 years
Hereditary disorders:	Parents and pups should be eye-tested
Hip dysplasia:	16 (breed mean score)

Suitability

Exercise:	Plenty of exercise with free running and play is a must
Ease of training:	Very easy, but as they're very intelligent, they have an independent streak
Temperament with children:	Very good
With dogs?	Good with all breeds
With cats?	Okay with own, may chase others
Town or country dog?	Country
Would he happily live in a flat or apartment?	They can, but must be exercised - they need mental stimulation
Natural guard dog?	Yes
Attitude to strangers?	Suspicious

Want to know more?

Breed advice: Ian Crowther 01837 52439; Mrs S Hopgood 01773 534820; Joy Crowther 01276 472828
Breed rescue: Joy Crowther 01276 472828; Louise Grover 01324 810753

Special considerations
When working, smooth-coated dogs will tolerate the cold, but they need warmth when off-duty. Wires tolerate the weather better. Take special care to keep the ears clean.

Like this?
Check out these alternatives:

- Weimaraner
- German Shorthaired Pointer
- German Wirehaired Pointer

History

When Magyar tribes migrated westward from eastern Europe, they brought their versatile hunting dogs with them. During the Middle Ages, the influence of the Magyars extended well beyond the borders of modern-day Hungary. The Vizsla is a multicultural dog, with ancestors from Turkey and Transylvania, and it is closely related to its German cousin, the Weimaraner. Arguments rumble on as to which came first, but it doesn't really matter either way.

In the 19th century, a distinctive breed began to emerge, and, by the early 1940s, there were around 5,000 registered pedigree Vizslas in Hungary. But after the dark days of the Second World War, only a handful remained. Fortunately, some had been taken out of the country by emigrants, and a salvage operation rescued the breed from oblivion. Today, the Vizsla is once again a popular companion in his native homeland.

Character sketch

A lively, athletic, fun-loving dog, who is devoted to his family. Will work and play with equal enthusiasm. However, caution should be exercised with small children - this is a sensitive breed that is not willing to put up with rough handling. He may be a hunting dog, but the Hungarian Vizsla loves his family and loves also to lie in front of the fire with his owner. An ideal all-round companion, this breed is not easily bettered.

Vital statistics

Height:	53-64 cms
Weight:	20-30 kgs
Exercise:	●●●●
Grooming:	●○○○
Noise:	●●○○
Food bill:	£7.50 per week

Country of origin:	Hungary
Original function:	Hunt, point, retrieve gundog
Availability:	Difficult

Colours:	Russet gold
Coat type:	Smooth or wire
Coat care:	The smooth coat needs cleaning with a hound glove and polishing; the wire needs a weekly brush and comb, as well as after a country walk

Health

Average life span:	14 years
Hereditary disorders:	Parents and pups should be eye-tested
Hip dysplasia:	12 (breed mean score)

Suitability

Exercise:	As much as possible, with plenty of free-running and games to stimulate the mind
Ease of training:	Fairly easy
Temperament with children:	Good, if treated with respect; bite inhibition training is essential
With dogs?	Generally good, though males can exhibit some arrogance towards others
With cats?	Okay, if socialised carefully
Town or country dog?	Prefers the country
Would he happily live in a flat or apartment?	If exercised adequately
Natural guard dog?	No, but is watchful and will bark at anything unusual
Attitude to strangers?	Not particularly suspicious

Want to know more?

Breed advice: Jim & Sharon Bergin 01400 251825
Breed rescue: Sue Millson 01892 834178; Claire Aldridge 01959 573317

Irish Setter *(left margin)*

Like this?
Check out these alternatives:

- Gordon Setter
- Flat Coated Retriever
- English Springer Spaniel

Character sketch

An energetic and intelligent breed that needs a combination of exercise and play to stimulate his body and mind. The breed was originally developed to work in the field, where they needed to be quick and agile. The Irish Setter is a real athlete!

Special considerations

Do not allow him to get fat. This 'people dog' hates being left. An Irish Setter who is shut up all day will soon become miserable and possibly destructive.

History

Texts from the 16th century refer to a 'setting spaniel' - setting dogs had the task of finding the game and then freezing the bird on the spot so that huntsmen could throw a net over it.

The Irish Setter Club settled on a breed standard in 1886, and the breed made a great splash at shows in the UK and the US, and became a popular family pet. Unfortunately, such an energetic dog did not always fit into city life, and they gained a reputation for being 'difficult'. Fashions change, however, which is probably fortunate for the Irish Setter. They may be less common than they once were, but they are now more likely to be owned by people who understand that there's more to these dogs than a pretty coat.

Irish Red & White Setters

Most Irish Setters were originally parti-colour, yet in the mid 1850s the fashion changed to solid colours and the Red and Whites nearly died out. The colouration was saved in the 1920s, and by the 1940s they were recognised as a separate breed.

Vital statistics

Height:	63-69 cms
Weight:	27-32 kgs, depending on height
Exercise:	●●●●
Grooming:	●●○○
Noise:	●●○○
Food bill:	£8 per week

Country of origin:	Ireland
Original function:	Setting game birds for shooters
Availability:	Easy

Colours:	Rich red chestnut
Coat type:	Silky, flat, and as free of wave or curl as possible
Coat care:	A thorough brush and comb through twice a week. Pay particular attention to feathering, armpits and behind the ears

Health

Average life span:	12 years
Hereditary disorders:	Parents should be eye-tested and tested for CLAD - an immune system disease
Hip dysplasia:	15 (breed mean score)

Suitability

Exercise:	At least two 45-minute walks a day, with some daily free-running
Ease of training:	Can be trained to a high level with the right motivation
Temperament with children:	Excellent, but they can be too boisterous for little ones
With dogs?	Very good
With cats?	Okay with 'own' if socialised when young
Town or country dog?	Prefers the country, but can be flexible
Would he happily live in a flat or apartment?	No
Natural guard dog?	No - but he might bark a warning
Attitude to strangers?	Generally friendly

Want to know more?

 Breed advice: Cheryl Stevenson 01827 701890; Maureen Hurll 01787 248143; Mrs Brigden 01342 312964
Breed rescue: Barbara Rogers 01625 872708

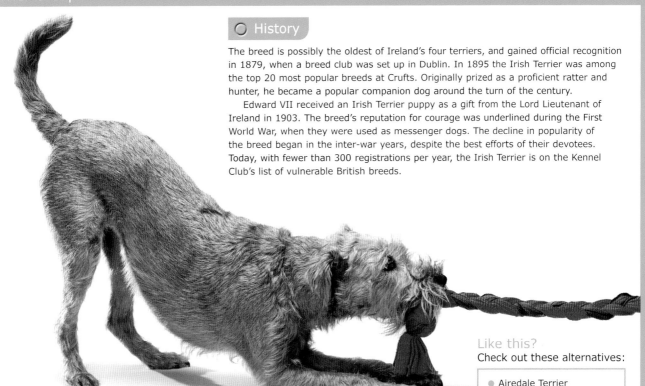

History

The breed is possibly the oldest of Ireland's four terriers, and gained official recognition in 1879, when a breed club was set up in Dublin. In 1895 the Irish Terrier was among the top 20 most popular breeds at Crufts. Originally prized as a proficient ratter and hunter, he became a popular companion dog around the turn of the century.

Edward VII received an Irish Terrier puppy as a gift from the Lord Lieutenant of Ireland in 1903. The breed's reputation for courage was underlined during the First World War, when they were used as messenger dogs. The decline in popularity of the breed began in the inter-war years, despite the best efforts of their devotees. Today, with fewer than 300 registrations per year, the Irish Terrier is on the Kennel Club's list of vulnerable British breeds.

Like this?
Check out these alternatives:

- Airedale Terrier
- Border Terrier
- Parson Russell Terrier
- Belgian Shepherd Dog (Laekenois)

Character sketch

A loving companion, outgoing and inquisitive, full of happiness, the Irish Terrier is one of the great characters of the dog world. Their affection and loyalty will extend to the whole family. When out walking, though, be very vigilant around other dogs, as the Irish Terrier is quick to take offence and the size of the offender makes no difference - he is courageous in the face of any challenge.

Special considerations
Good, thorough socialisation from puppyhood is essential, as are training classes. Recall training can be difficult, and though your 'Red Devil' will enjoy free-running, he should only be let off-lead well away from traffic.

Vital statistics

Height:	46-48 cms
Weight:	16-20 kgs
Exercise:	●●○○
Grooming:	●●●○
Noise:	●○○○
Food bill:	£5 per week

Country of origin:	Ireland
Original function:	Vermin control on farms
Availability:	Moderate

Colours:	Red, red-wheaten, or yellow-red
Coat type:	Harsh and wiry, with a soft undercoat
Coat care:	If muddy, a quick brush through. Once or twice a year, the coat should be handstripped, though some pet owners clip for convenience

Health

Average life span:	14 years
Hereditary disorders:	None known to breeders
Hip dysplasia:	Insufficient numbers have been tested

Suitability

Exercise:	A reasonable daily walk is recommended, plus play in the garden
Ease of training:	Not the easiest, but success can be achieved with firm, patient, kind training
Temperament with children:	Good, provided the children are taught to respect dogs
With dogs?	Be careful, particularly with males
With cats?	Exercise great care; puppies can usually be socialised to accept the family cat
Town or country dog?	Prefers country life but will adapt
Would he happily live in a flat or apartment?	Not ideal, though it's possible if he's exercised adequately
Natural guard dog?	Yes
Attitude to strangers?	Suspicious initially

Want to know more?

Breed advice: Miss A Bradley 01733 205386; Jonathan & Claire Hyde 07977 629354; Ian A Hardman 01204 436224
Breed rescue: Jill Looker 01264 850255

History

Spaniel-like dogs trained to retrieve from water were known in Roman times, and descendants of these dogs found their way to Spain and Portugal and, eventually, to the Emerald Isle. But the more immediate origin of the breed does not involve Roman togas or hot weather!

The Irish Water Spaniel we know today emerged in Ireland in the 1830s, when spaniels were divided according to use and were known as either land or water spaniels. The IWS probably developed from both the South Country Water Spaniel and the North Country Water Spaniel, with a bit of Portuguese Water Spaniel (hence the long history) and some Poodle thrown in (the IWS has been described as a "stocky Poodle").

Folk tales of IWS performing daring rescues in the water abound in Ireland. Today these dogs are rare - in fact, with fewer than 300 registrations per year, they are on the Kennel Club's list of vulnerable British and Irish breeds.

Character sketch

This is a very active, fun dog, with a good sense of humour. He is highly intelligent, loves human companionship and enjoys being a bit of a clown. As you would expect, the Irish Water Spaniel is a strong swimmer and great retriever in the water - you could well find yourself living with an almost permanently wet dog.

Special considerations

He needs firm but considerate training from young. The breed can be prone to putting on weight, so watch the amount of food given. Needs mental stimulation as well as lots of exercise. The coat will pick up all sorts on a walk - burrs, grass seeds, twigs. But at least the mud doesn't show up on that glorious liver coat!

Like this?
Check out these alternatives:

- Portuguese Water Dog
- Afghan Hound
- Curly Coated Retriever
- Bedlington Terrier

Vital statistics

Height:	51-58 cms
Weight:	27-32 kgs
Exercise:	●●●○
Grooming:	●●●○
Noise:	●●○○
Food bill:	£8 per week

Country of origin:	Ireland
Original function:	Gundog
Availability:	Difficult

Colours:	A rich dark liver with a purplish tint
Coat type:	Dense, tight, crisp ringlets
Coat care:	A weekly brush and comb is needed to keep the coat in top condition

Health

Average life span:	12 years
Hereditary disorders:	None known to breeders
Hip dysplasia:	17 (breed mean score)

Suitability

Exercise:	As much as you can give - he will take a lot of exercise or will accept two or three short walks a day
Ease of training:	Good
Temperament with children:	Good, but must be well socialised from puppyhood
With dogs?	Good
With cats?	Okay
Town or country dog?	Mainly country
Would he happily live in a flat or apartment?	With proper exercise and mental stimulation
Natural guard dog?	A good watchdog
Attitude to strangers?	Can be reserved

Want to know more?

Breed advice & rescue: Mrs Chris Attwood 01526 322081

Character sketch

A highly intelligent, very active breed, at home working in virtually all types of terrain, open field or forest, lake or marshland, or the arid rocky terrain of northern Italy - this dog can do it all. A supreme all-round gundog, an affectionate and loyal companion, and a popular show dog.

Special considerations
Buy only from breeders who hip-score and who explain to you the history of cerebellar ataxia. This breed tends to put on weight easily, so be careful to give the correct amount of food.

History

The Spinone can be regarded as a truly ancient breed, with origins possibly as far back as the 13th century, probably with traces of the even more ancient and indigenous Italian hound breed, the Segugio Italiano.

There would have been little selective breeding before 1828, when the breed was first described in print. The name 'Spinone' derives from a particularly prickly bush, very common in parts of northern Italy, called the 'pino', into which only a Spinone would throw himself in the pursuit of game!

The breed saw active service in the two World Wars, and in the 1912 Tripoli campaign, where his prowess as a tracker was put to good use by the military. At the end of the Second World War, though, numbers in his native Italy had been decimated, and the Spinone was virtually unknown outside northern Italy. The breed was in danger of being lost forever, until breeders began a concerted effort during the 1950s to reconstruct the Spinone Italiano, as there was still demand for a large, powerful, all-round gundog.

Like this?
Check out these alternatives:

- German Wirehaired Pointer
- Schnauzer
- Weimaraner
- Otterhound

Vital statistics

Height:	58-70 cms
Weight:	29-39 kgs
Exercise:	●●●○
Grooming:	●●●●○
Noise:	●●○○
Food bill:	About £7 per week

Country of origin:	Italy
Original function:	Hunt, point and retrieve
Availability:	Moderate. If you are prepared to travel, you shouldn't have any difficulty
Colours:	White, white with orange or brown markings, or brown roan (flecked)
Coat type:	A harsh outercoat; no undercoat should be present
Coat care:	A thorough groom once a week

Health

Average life span:	11 years
Hereditary disorders:	Elbow dysplasia. DNA test for cerebellar ataxia available
Hip dysplasia:	14 (breed mean score)

Suitability

Exercise:	Exercise adult dogs until you are exhausted - and then do it again!
Ease of training:	Easy to moderate. They can be stubborn
Temperament with children:	Extremely good
With dogs?	Affable
With cats?	Good with 'own' cats but take care with others
Town or country dog?	Country
Would he happily live in a flat or apartment?	No
Natural guard dog?	No
Attitude to strangers?	Friendly

Want to know more?

Breed advice: Gaynor Killick 01985 218161; Mary Potter 01386 438040; Janet Neil 01209 890630
Breed rescue: Gillie Gormasall 01284 735222

Character sketch

This is a complicated breed, needing a kind, resourceful owner. They can be stubborn, aloof and difficult to train.

Special considerations

This dog is very self-willed and has a unique scream if annoyed. Dislikes being handled by strangers; early socialisation and training are musts. He loves his food, so ensure he doesn't become obese. Can suffer a kidney ailment if fed too high a protein diet. During the twice-yearly moult, you will find hair literally everywhere.

Like this?
Check out these alternatives:

- Akita
- Basenji
- Samoyed
- Japanese Spitz

History

Remains of small dogs dating back thousands of years testify to the ancient lineage of the Shiba's ancestors. It seems likely that dogs arrived in Japan around 7000BC. Later arrivals added other varieties of dog to the mix and it's thought that European breeds, such as setters and pointers, were eventually crossed with Japanese breeds. These hardy, country dogs were used to flush birds and other game. Japan was closed to foreigners throughout the 17th and 18th centuries, so its dogs - like many other aspects of its culture - remained unknown.

As Japan opened up to the world during the 19th century, imported breeds of dog became popular, and by the beginning of the 20th century, the survival of some of Japan's indigenous breeds was looking uncertain. In 1928, an organisation was set up to help protect them. The Second World War and an epidemic of distemper that followed it left the Shiba's future in doubt. It is thought that only three bloodlines survived, but since then the Shiba has recovered remarkably well and is today the fourth most popular pedigree in Japan.

Vital statistics

Height:	36.5-39.5 cms
Weight:	7-10 kgs
Exercise:	●○○○
Grooming:	●●○○
Noise:	●○○○
Food bill:	About £8 per week

Country of origin:	Japan
Original function:	Hunting small game and birds
Availability:	Not easy

Colours:	Red, black and tan, sesame (red with black tipping), and white
Coat type:	Thick, dense, soft undercoat and a thick, harsh, weather-resisting topcoat
Coat care:	Groom once or twice a day when moulting. Other times, just every week or so

Health

Average life span:	18 years
Hereditary disorders:	Patella luxation. Parents should be eye-tested
Hip dysplasia:	10 (breed mean score)

Suitability

Exercise:	Minimum of two half-hour walks a day
Ease of training:	Not easy. Patience and kindness needed
Temperament with children:	Excellent with respectful children
With dogs?	Some can be very difficult unless trained and socialised from puppyhood
With cats?	Okay with family's cats, if raised with them. With other cats - be very careful!
Town or country dog?	Either, provided sufficiently stimulated
Would he happily live in a flat or apartment?	No
Natural guard dog?	No, but he's watchful and will warn
Attitude to strangers?	Aloof initially

Want to know more?

Breed advice: Miriam Clews 01707 883711; Janice Bannister 01952 613500
Breed rescue: Gill Bingham 01384 214868

Character sketch

A very affectionate and curious little dog who wants to be with his family every minute. He is highly intelligent and has enormous stamina, but is adaptable and will live happily in a town, as long as he has sufficient exercise. He is territorial and tends to distrust strangers. Loves children and makes a good family dog.

Special considerations

He hates to be left alone. Can be noisy, and will give a warning every time he hears an unusual noise. Coat care is not for the faint-hearted, and this breed will not suit the house-proud, as the hair sheds continually.

History

The origins of the Japanese Spitz are truly mysterious. Any history of this fascinating breed was eliminated during the Second World War. Although the breed is included in the list of the 10 Japanese breeds, it is doubtful that its origin lies there. A quick glance reminds you of breeds like the Samoyed and German Spitz, but the development of the breed is entirely Japanese. It is said that several large white spitz-type dogs were imported into Japan in the 1920s and 30s, from Siberia, north-eastern China and Canada. Fanciers began to selectively breed for smaller specimens, eventually producing a miniature version of the Samoyed or German Spitz. After the Second World War the breed was on the edge of extinction and great efforts were needed to restore it. These were successful, and the Japanese Kennel Club established the breed standard in 1948.

Like this?
Check out these alternatives:

- German Spitz (Mittel)
- Bichon Frise
- Papillon
- Samoyed
- Tibetan Spaniel

Vital statistics

Height:	30-37 cms
Weight:	7-8 kgs
Exercise:	●●○○
Grooming:	●●●○
Noise:	●●○○
Food bill:	About £5 per week

Country of origin:	Japan
Original function:	Watchdog and companion
Availability:	Difficult

Colours:	Pure white
Coat type:	Outer harsh coat, straight/standoff, profuse; soft, dense undercoat
Coat care:	Combing twice a week, every day when moulting. The coat mats easily and sheds continually

Health

Average life span:	14 years
Hereditary disorders:	Patella luxation
Hip dysplasia:	Insufficient numbers have been tested

Suitability

Exercise:	Two good walks daily, or will take as much as the owner wants
Ease of training:	Good, but needs patience
Temperament with children:	Excellent providing children are not too heavy handed
With dogs?	Good
With cats?	Okay with family's cats, if raised with them. Take care with others
Town or country dog?	Either
Would he happily live in a flat or apartment?	With company and exercise, yes
Natural guard dog?	A natural watchdog, will warn
Attitude to strangers?	Suspicious

Want to know more?

Breed advice: Janet Weller 01684 773423
Breed rescue: Mrs Moody 01628 548813

History

The Keeshond is a member of the European spitz family. Despite having once been known as 'the Dutch barge dog' and affectionately named 'the smiling Dutchman', the Fédération Cynologique Internationale insists that the Keeshond is, in fact, identical to the Wolfspitz and is properly a German breed. While not everyone is in agreement with this, it is clear that all these dogs are very closely related.

The Keeshond is named after Cornelis de Gyselaer, who was the leader of a rebellion against the House of Orange in the late 18th century. The House of Orange was closely associated with the Pug, so Cornelis took up this small but tenacious breed as a symbol of the rebels' cause. Kees was Cornelis' nickname and the dog came to be known as 'the dog of Kees', or Keeshond.

They worked on farms as watchdogs and companions and were often seen on barges, where they kept a look-out and controlled vermin. Some of these dogs found their way to Britain in the early 20th century, but today the breed is still fairly obscure - both in the UK and in the Netherlands.

Like this?
Check out these alternatives:

- German Spitz (Klein and Mittel)
- Japanese Spitz
- Pomeranian
- Samoyed

Character sketch

Gentle and loyal with a sense of fun. Devoted to their human family, these dogs like nothing better than to be with their loved ones and are friendly and outgoing dogs.

Special considerations
The Keeshond is not a dog for those who want blind obedience - it is a spitz! The double coat is not hard to maintain, but owners need to be prepared to groom thoroughly.

Vital statistics

Height:	43-46 cms
Weight:	15-20 kgs
Exercise:	●●●○
Grooming:	●●●○
Noise:	●●●○
Food bill:	About £7 per week

Country of origin:	Holland (and Germany)
Original function:	Barge dog, vermin control, watchdog
Availability:	Difficult
Colours:	Grey/black topcoat with pale grey or cream undercoat. Body hairs tipped black, spectacle-like markings around the eyes
Coat type:	Harsh off-standing, weatherproof outer coat, and dense, soft, pale undercoat
Coat care:	A thorough brush through twice a week

Health

Average life span:	13 years
Hereditary disorders:	Some heart problems. DNA test available for a metabolic problem
Hip dysplasia:	12 (breed mean score)

Suitability

Exercise:	Around half an hour's exercise a day, with free-running and play in the garden
Ease of training:	Quick to learn, respond well to rewards
Temperament with children:	They have a special affinity with children and make excellent family dogs
With dogs?	Good
With cats?	Many are okay after careful introductions
Town or country dog?	Will live happily in either
Would he happily live in a flat or apartment?	Not ideal, but they will adapt as long as they are taken out regularly for exercise
Natural guard dog?	A good watchdog - he has acute hearing
Attitude to strangers?	Initially aloof with strangers. Friends are given enthusiastic welcomes

Want to know more?

Breed advice: Margaret Foster & Winne Pearson 01469 531068; Mrs Henman 01604 831974
Breed rescue: Jeane Waller 01293 516284

Character sketch

Doodle puppies are hyperactive, so an owner must give time to their education. It is not possible to predict the type of coat that will develop. If it leans toward the Poodle type, it will not moult; if more like a Labrador, it will moult. If it's a mixture, it will be anyone's guess.

Labradoodles can be super pets, provided you know what the breed needs and are able to provide an active life. They are highly perceptive, and full of fun, revelling in taking part in the family's activities.

Special considerations

This dog does not like to be left alone - he'll find ways of expressing his dislike if left.

A leading breeder says that if you are not at home all day, don't bother getting a Labradoodle! Being highly intelligent, they need their brains stimulated.

The hair inside the ears should be removed; it grows thickly and swiftly. Care should be taken to keep the beard clean.

Like this?
Check out these alternatives:

- Curly Coated Retriever
- Irish Water Spaniel
- Labrador Retriever
- Poodle

History

The Labradoodle's history is still very much in the making. Sometimes dismissively described as a 'designer dog', while on other occasions lauded as the perfect pooch, the Doodle, like many other breeds, was developed with a very specific purpose in mind.

In the 1980s, the Australian Guide Dog Association deliberately crossed a Labrador with a Poodle. The idea was that the Labrador's trustworthy, trainable qualities, combined with the Poodle's non-shedding coat, would produce a guide dog suitable for people with allergies.

The Australian Labradoodle Association has drawn up a breed standard, which describes three sizes and two coat types.

Vital statistics

Height:	35.5-76 cms
Weight:	7.5-38 kgs
Exercise:	●●●○
Grooming:	●●○○
Noise:	●●○○
Food bill:	£7 to £10 per week

Country of origin:	Australia
Original function:	Service dog
Availability:	Not easy

Colours:	Every dog coat colour; particolours are now beginning to crop up in the UK
Coat type:	Can vary from the springy, Poodle type to the flat, Labrador type
Coat care:	Lab-type coat: weekly brush through. Fleecy, soft, wavy coats need trimming.

Health

Average life span:	11 years
Hereditary disorders:	Eye-test parents. DNA test for blood-clotting disorder and skin disorder
Hip dysplasia:	14 (breed mean score)

Suitability

Exercise:	Two half-hour walks, with free-running and play in the garden, will suffice
Ease of training:	Easy - these dogs are bright and willing to learn with the correct motivation
Temperament with children:	Good with respectful children
With dogs?	Good, but they can get over-excited!
With cats?	Okay with adequate socialisation
Town or country dog?	Prefers country, but will adapt to town
Would he happily live in a flat or apartment?	Yes, if he was properly stimulated, physically and mentally
Natural guard dog?	No, but will generally warn of strangers
Attitude to strangers?	Most are eager to meet, but some aloof

Want to know more?

Breed advice: Annette Connolly-Read 020 8894 1613; Carol and Andy Gowling 01768 341380
Breed rescue: Annette Courtney 01234 782809

Labrador Retriever

History

There is talk that the Labrador emanated from Greenland, taken to Newfoundland in the 10th century by none other than the Viking Eric the Red. A theory with a stronger base is that the breed originated from Dorset and travelled to Newfoundland with trading vessels.

What is certain is that in the early 18th century there was a water dog already in the region, known as the St John's Newfoundland, which could have been a descendant of the Viking dogs.

Major Maurice Portal, a great authority on the breed in those days, wrote of the probability that the Pointer was introduced, which eventually achieved the hard- and short-coated dog.

It was probably these dogs that attracted attention from Lord Malmesbury, who had a place not far from Poole. He is credited with being the first owner of these dogs around the year 1809.

Like this?
Check out these alternatives:

- Chesapeake Bay Retriever
- Curly Coated Retriever
- Flat Coated Retriever
- Golden Retriever

Special considerations
Very good eaters, keep control of weight. Do not excessively exercise before six months old.

Character sketch

An active, good-tempered, intelligent, adaptable family pet - very kind without aggression or shyness. Not suitable for everybody; because of their excess energy and mental independence, they can be a handful unless trained from young. Get it all right and you'll have a magnificent friend who thinks he's human and will want to be included in all family activities.

As a gundog, his strength, stamina and enthusiasm are outstanding. These attributes, together with his sense of smell and retrieving capabilities, particularly in water, make him the greatest working gundog of all time.

Vital statistics

Height:	55-57 cms
Weight:	27 kgs plus
Exercise:	●●●○
Grooming:	●○○○
Noise:	●○○○
Food bill:	£8 per week

Country of origin:	Newfoundland
Original function:	Retriever
Availability:	Easy

Colours:	Black, yellow, liver/chocolate, - white spot on chest permissible
Coat type:	Short, dense, straight - waterproof undercoat
Coat care:	A weekly brush to remove loose hairs is all that is needed

Health

Average life span:	12 years
Hereditary disorders:	Eye-test parents and pups. DNA tests for narcolepsy and muscular disorder
Hip dysplasia:	15 (breed mean score)

Suitability

Exercise:	As much as you can manage when adult. Keep to a minimum until six months old and gradually increase
Ease of training:	Moderate to easy. Anxious to please
Temperament with children:	Excellent
With dogs?	Invariably good
With cats?	Not aggressive
Town or country dog?	Country
Would he happily live in a flat or apartment?	Could live in a flat with frequent exercise
Natural guard dog?	No, but will give warning of strangers
Attitude to strangers?	Friendly

Want to know more?

Breed advice: Josephine Mulqueen 01638 714560; Mrs J Green 01732 823321; Erica Down 01228 791382
Breed rescue: Mrs Latchford 01277 226587; Mrs Pratt 01278 685815

History

The Large Munsterlander is a German breed developed in the latter half of the 18th century as an all-purpose gundog. Most of the German gundogs had their origins in the very old hunting breeds known as 'Schweisshund', big, slow scent hounds of mixed ancestry.

It is fairly easy to discern some of the breeds behind the Large Munsterlander. Setters spring to mind, but the father of the breed is said to be the German Longhaired Pointer, which may have had in its background the Irish Setter, the Newfoundland and the Gordon Setter among others.

By 1919 the Large Munsterlander was fully accepted and registered as a separate breed, but it wasn't until 1971 that six dogs were imported into the UK.

Like this?
Check out these alternatives:

- German Longhaired Pointer
- Gordon Setter
- Irish Red and White Setter
- Welsh Springer Spaniel

Character sketch

The original German breeders looked for a dog that not only could perform its role as a hunting dog, but could double as a general farm dog, guarding the property and family.

Highly intelligent, they love games in the garden like 'hunt the toy' but will be equally ready for a stroll to the pub in the evening. A word of warning, however: this is strictly a 'people dog', who dislikes being left alone. They love their family dearly and want to be involved in all activities.

If you can be with them for much of the time, there are few breeds to match them.

Special considerations
These dogs object loudly to being left alone. They have an extremely active nature and should have human company and things to do.

Vital statistics

Height:	58-65 cms
Weight:	25-29 kgs
Exercise:	●●●○
Grooming:	●●●○
Noise:	●●○○
Food bill:	£7.50 a week

Country of origin:	Germany
Original function:	Hunt, point and retrieve
Availability:	Difficult
Colours:	Solid black head, small, thin white blaze permitted (but not desirable). Body white or blue roan, black patches, flecked, ticked or combination of these
Coat type:	Fine, reasonably silky, not much undercoat
Coat care:	Weekly brush and comb

Health

Average life span:	11 years
Hereditary disorders:	Eye-test parents
Hip dysplasia:	13 (breed mean score)

Suitability

Exercise:	A busy dog that needs to be well exercised
Ease of training:	Easy but needs patient training; likes to please
Temperament with children:	Excellent
With dogs?	No problems
With cats?	No problems with own, take care with others
Town or country dog?	Country
Would he happily live in a flat or apartment?	It wouldn't be fair to keep this dog in a flat
Natural guard dog?	Yes, but not aggressive
Attitude to strangers?	Not suspicious

Want to know more?

Breed advice: Elizabeth Tyson 01427 628256
Breed rescue: Rae Massey 01302 711691

Leonberger

History

In 1846 Herr Essig was the mayor of Leonberg in Germany who bred dogs as a sideline. In translation 'Leonberg' breaks down into two words: 'leon' equates to 'lion', and 'berg' means 'mountain'. Leonberg's coat of arms featured two lions, but as lions were a bit light on the ground in Germany, Herr Essig conceived the idea of breeding a dog that looked like a lion.

Essig went to the St Bernard Hospice on the Pass of St Bernard between France and Switzerland, famous for its St Bernard dogs, to mate a bitch. He added Landseer Newfoundland blood and acquired a Pyrenean Mountain Dog.

The antecedents of the Leonberger are working breeds and have been used as search and rescue dogs, possibly an inheritance from the St Bernard. They are also powerful swimmers - perhaps a legacy from the Newfoundland.

Like this?
Check out these alternatives:

- Bernese Mountain Dog
- Newfoundland
- Pyrenean Mountain Dog
- St Bernard
- Tibetan Mastiff

Character sketch

A gentle, loving softie, the Leonberger is very laid-back and companionable. If they have early socialisation and are integrated into activities, they will become a member of the family, but they do need kindness. They seem particularly sympathetic to both the young and old.

Being a big dog, he eats a lot, but care should be taken not to let him get fat, as without stimulation he will be a couch potato. He will respond to loving attention and training and become a friend of which any family would be proud.

Special considerations
They do not like being left alone and need plenty of mental stimulation.

Vital statistics

Height:	65-80 cms
Weight:	40-50 kgs
Exercise:	●●○○
Grooming:	●●●○
Noise:	●○○○
Food bill:	£12.50 per week

Country of origin:	Germany
Original function:	Companion
Availability:	Difficult

Colours:	Light yellow, golden to red-brown with black mask. Dark or black points acceptable
Coat type:	Medium to harsh, fairly long and close despite a thick undercoat. Evident mane
Coat care:	Regular brushing and combing

Health

Average life span:	10 years
Hereditary disorders:	Elbow dysplasia. Parents should be eye-tested
Hip dysplasia:	12 (breed mean score)

Suitability

Exercise:	Minimum of one hour daily, plus play in the garden with free-running
Ease of training:	Very easy
Temperament with children:	Most excellent
With dogs?	Normally friendly
With cats?	No problems
Town or country dog?	Country
Would he happily live in a flat or apartment?	With exercise and TLC
Natural guard dog?	A watchdog
Attitude to strangers?	Friendly

Want to know more?

 Breed advice: Liz Guy-Halke 01379 853365; K Hay 01375 891488
Breed rescue: Midge Clayton 01205 260692

The Löwchen is related to the Bichon family that has always been bred primarily as companions.

The English name is adopted from German (Löwchen means 'little lion'), but the Fédération Cynologique Internationale lists it as a French breed and it has also been described as a native of Russia. But this is an ancient breed: much older than any of these countries.

The trade in small companion dogs began in the pre-modern era, when sailors crossed the Mediterranean.

The mass distribution of dogs was picked up again in earnest by Spanish sailors in the 15th century. Traders sold their wares, including dogs, across the rapidly developing civilisations of Renaissance Europe.

There are scores of paintings from the 15th, 16th and 17th centuries, which testify to the popularity of small, fluffy dogs - many with the trademark Löwchen lion cut - among aristocratic Europeans.

Character sketch

A highly intelligent dog that is easily trained, the Löwchen is a happy, playful companion.

He is frisky, amusing, and, in many ways, the ideal pet dog: he's small enough to be lifted, he doesn't eat a lot, and he's very affectionate.

The Löwchen loves nothing more than contact with his humans. He will play happily with the children and will love to be involved in family activities. Then, at the end of an exhausting day, he will lie on the lap of anyone who'll have him.

Special considerations

Avoid tangling by combing the coat daily. Dry him thoroughly after walks and be careful not to overfeed.

Like this?
Check out these alternatives:

- Bichon Frise
- Bolognese
- Havanese
- Maltese
- Tibetan Terrier

Vital statistics

Height:	25-33 cms
Weight:	4.5-5.5 kgs
Exercise:	●●○○
Grooming:	●●●●
Noise:	●●●○
Food bill:	£2 a week

Country of origin:	Primarily France
Original function:	Companion
Availability:	Not easy

Colours:	Any colour or combination
Coat type:	Long, wavy, fine and silky
Coat care:	A daily comb and brush is needed if he is in show cut; every other day will suffice if he is in a pet 'puppy' cut

Health

Average life span:	14 years
Hereditary disorders:	Patella luxation
Hip dysplasia:	14 (breed mean score)

Suitability

Exercise:	Two half-hour walks a day, together with quality play
Ease of training:	Easy
Temperament with children:	Excellent - but children must be trained how to behave around dogs
With dogs?	No problems
With cats?	Fine, if he's brought up with them
Town or country dog?	Either
Would he happily live in a flat or apartment?	Yes, if adequately exercised
Natural guard dog?	No, but he's very watchful and will warn if something unusual happens
Attitude to strangers?	Friendly

Want to know more?

Breed advice: Sue Terry 01673 858044
Breed rescue: Janet Edwards 01746 862507

Maltese

History

The island of Malta has a long, rich history. The Phoenicians, who came from the Mediterranean coast of what is now Lebanon, dominated sea trade in the first millennium BC and occupied Malta. As well as spices and metals, the Phoenicians traded dogs.

Of course, there's no hard evidence to prove that the Maltese actually came from Malta, and there are claims that the Maltese has an Asian background.

A 2004 research paper from the Canine Studies Institute identified 10 prototype canines believed to be the ancestors of the hundreds of breeds we have today. The Maltese - with an estimated history dating back to 3000BC - was named as the prototype toy.

There are suggestions that the Romans may have brought Maltese-type dogs to Britain in 55BC but hard evidence of early-day Maltese dogs doesn't emerge until the 1500s.

Character sketch

He has great fondness for his owners, and loves being involved in family activities. This is a fun, active dog, with a great sense of humour.

They are intelligent, and, despite their size, will protect their owners - they have no sense of their smallness. They have a sensitive nature and can be sulky if they think they are being hard done by. These exuberant dogs love to run free, and their ability to jump can be spectacular.

Special considerations

The Maltese hates boarding kennels and will pine for his owners. Children must be taught to be gentle, as he can be easily hurt.

Like this?

Check out these alternatives:

- Bichon Frise
- Bolognese
- Havanese
- Yorkshire Terrier

Vital statistics

Height:	25 cms
Weight:	2.7-3.2 kgs
Exercise:	●○○○
Grooming:	●●●●
Noise:	●○○○
Food bill:	Under £6 a week

Country of origin:	Mediterranean
Original function:	Companion
Availability:	Moderate

Colours:	An all white coat is preferred, but a slight lemon colour is permitted
Coat type:	Long and silky, with no undercoat
Coat care:	A daily, gentle brush and comb is essential

Health

Average life span:	15 years
Hereditary disorders:	Patella luxation
Hip dysplasia:	Insufficient numbers have been tested

Suitability

Exercise:	Two or three 20-minute walks a day will suffice, though they will walk for longer
Ease of training:	Moderate
Temperament with children:	Very good
With dogs?	Very good
With cats?	Okay if socialised early enough
Town or country dog?	Either, but he can lose his coat whiteness in towns!
Would he happily live in a flat or apartment?	Yes, with adequate exercise
Natural guard dog?	No, but they will warn vociferously
Attitude to strangers?	Friendly

Want to know more?

Breed advice & rescue: Carol Hemsley 01276 857786

Character sketch

A fearless little dog who is full of confidence, the Min Pin makes a super companion. Min Pins enjoy being part of their owners' lives and will join in with most activities.

Min Pins are generally good with other animals, but, being terrier-like, they will chase rabbits and even birds, unless trained to leave them.

They are feisty, loyal and intelligent and will guard you or their possessions. They are good watch dogs, but sometimes they don't know when to stop telling you that someone is at the door!

Special considerations

Nails should be kept short; long nails can cause stress to the foot. Special care should be taken with teeth, to promote good health, and dogs should become accustomed to having their teeth cleaned on a regular basis from puppyhood.

Like this?
Check out these alternatives:

- Affenpinscher
- Chihuahua
- Dobermann Pinscher
- German Pinscher

History

Although the breed, or something like it, was known in Germany at least 300 years ago, the Miniature Pinscher was not recognised as a distinct breed until 1895. In the early days of German dog showing, around the mid 1800s, Pinschers were lumped together with Schnauzers - Schnauzers were regarded as wire-haired Pinschers.

The Pinscher family takes in the petite Affenpinscher as well as the more substantial Dobermann.

Today's Min Pins don't look much like a smooth-coated Schnauzer and it's possible that Italian Greyhounds were introduced into the mix at some point - which would explain the Min Pin's elegant trot. It's also been suggested that the Min Pin owes something to the Dachshund - a breed once much appreciated in Germany for its ratting skills.

Vital statistics

Height:	25-30 cms
Weight:	4-5 kgs
Exercise:	●○○○
Grooming:	●○○○
Noise:	●●○○
Food bill:	£5 per week

Country of origin:	Germany
Original function:	Ratter
Availability:	Not very easy

Colours:	Solid red of varying shades along with black, chocolate and blue - each with sharply defined tan markings
Coat type:	Smooth, short, hard and lustrous
Coat care:	Minimal! An occasional wipe with a damp chamois keeps his coat shiny

Health

Average life span:	14 years
Hereditary disorders:	Patella luxation
Hip dysplasia:	Insufficient numbers have been tested

Suitability

Exercise:	Two or three walks daily plus garden play
Ease of training:	Not the easiest to train, but can excel with the right motivation
Temperament with children:	Very good, but children should not pick him up in case they accidentally hurt him
With dogs?	Usually good
With cats?	Usually good if socialised from puppyhood. Will probably chase other people's cats that come into their garden
Town or country dog?	Either - he's very adaptable
Would he happily live in a flat or apartment?	Yes, with adequate exercise
Natural guard dog?	Yes, he's very alert and has acute hearing
Attitude to strangers?	Confident

Want to know more?

Breed advice: A Saxby 0114 233 3467
Breed rescue: Sue Colborne-Baber 01227 860220

Miniature Schnauzer

Special considerations

Don't overfeed - they are greedy dogs that can get fat. For their mental and physical health, they must have things to do. Regular coat care is essential.

History

The late 1800s and the early 1900s were periods of breeding experimentation; it is likely that the main ingredients of the Mini Schnauzer were the smaller Standard Schnauzers crossed with Affenpinschers.

The principal ancestor of both the Giant and the Mini Schnauzer is said to be the Standard, which has been around since the 15th century and was used as a general farm dog.

The black colour, which was prevalent in the early days and is becoming more popular, may have been derived from the Toy Spitz - or Pomeranian, as the breed is called today. The argument was that the larger Spitz was used in the development of the Standard Schnauzer, so there is no reason why the toy variety could not have been used for producing the small Schnauzer.

The first Minis were imported into Britain in 1928.

Like this?
Check out these alternatives:

- Affenpinscher
- Cairn Terrier
- Giant Schnauzer
- Standard Schnauzer
- West Highland White Terrier

Character sketch

This dog is lively, fun and full of humour. He adores taking part in family activities, and makes a loving, gentle friend.

Bright and intelligent, Minis are fun dogs; they learn simple domestic rules very quickly, and love nothing more than playing games with each other and with their owners. They soon understand their position in the hierarchy and will react quickly to their owners' moods.

Minis have acute hearing, letting owners know when people are about, but, on the whole, they are not too noisy.

Vital statistics

Height:	33-36 cms
Weight:	7-8 kgs
Exercise:	●●○○
Grooming:	●●●○
Noise:	●●○○
Food bill:	£3 per week

Country of origin:	Germany
Original function:	Farm dog
Availability:	Fairly easy

Colours:	Pepper and salt, black, black and silver
Coat type:	Wire-haired, with a soft undercoat
Coat care:	Weekly brush and comb, especially the furnishings, which tend to tangle. The body is handstripped; the head, chest, bottom and lower tummy can be clipped

Health

Average life span:	13½ years
Hereditary disorders:	Eye-test parents and pups. DNA test for a muscular disorder
Hip dysplasia:	13 (breed mean score)

Suitability

Exercise:	As much as possible, including free running and play
Ease of training:	Easy
Temperament with children:	Very good
With dogs?	No problems
With cats?	Okay with 'own' cats if socialised early; may chase others
Town or country dog?	Either
Would he happily live in a flat or apartment?	Yes, with proper exercise
Natural guard dog?	Yes
Attitude to strangers?	Suspicious

Want to know more?

Breed advice: Karen Carroll 01524 411220; Ingrid Young 01773 833331
Breed rescue: Jacky Durso 01376 563072; Janet Callow 0161 439 3233

Special considerations
**Not easy to rear.
He needs space and
plenty of human contact.
The coat needs regular
attention, and food must
be of the best quality.**

Like this?
Check out these
alternatives:

- Bernese Mountain Dog
- Labrador Retriever
- Leonberger
- St Bernard
- Tibetan Mastiff

History

This hard-worker was originally used in Newfoundland - the Canadian province that
gave the breed its name - to haul from sea to shore. It's not clear how Newfies got
to Canada. Some say they are related to dogs bred by the native Beothuk Eskimos;
others believe they are descendants of European 'bear dog' breeds that were
transported to Canadian ports by Norwegian, Basque or French sailors.

The oldest existing account of the breed dates back to 1732. The Newfoundland
came to these shores as a member of crew. When ships docked in British ports, sailors
would entertain the locals with a demonstration of the dog's retrieving abilities.

The Newfoundland soon earned the nickname 'life-saving dog' and built up a
reputation for plucking drowning seafarers out of choppy waters.

Character sketch

**A true gentle giant with bear-like proportions, 'benign' and 'friendly' are apt
words to describe this remarkable dog. Famed for his devotion to children,
this is a big softie that needs lots of TLC. He just loves to serve humans,
especially in the water, and will 'save' swimmers who are not in trouble!**

**Because of his size, it is advisable to train him to keep him under control.
He is intelligent, and responds well, but he must be trained with gentleness.**

**The Newfoundland is not a dog for everyone. He requires commitment
and space, but with care, he will rapidly become your pride and joy.**

Vital statistics

Height:	66-71 cms
Weight:	50-69 kgs
Exercise:	●●○○
Grooming:	●●●●
Noise:	●○○○
Food bill:	£10 per week

Country of origin:	Canada and Europe
Original function:	Farm- and water-worker
Availability:	Moderate

Colours:	Black, brown, or white with black markings (Landseer)
Coat type:	Double waterproof coat: thick, oily undercoat and thick, coarse, outer guard hair
Coat care:	A daily brush and comb.

Health

Average life span:	10 years
Hereditary disorders:	DNA test for a metabolic disorder
Hip dysplasia:	26 (breed mean score)

Suitability

Exercise:	Pups should not be over-exercised. Adults need two walks a day with a regular romp in the fields. Swimming, if possible
Ease of training:	Easy
Temperament with children:	Wonderful, provided children are wonderful with them
With dogs?	Very good, but males can be dominant
With cats?	No real problems if they are raised together
Town or country dog?	Prefers the country
Would he happily live in a flat or apartment?	Not really
Natural guard dog?	No, but a good deterrent
Attitude to strangers?	Friendly

Want to know more?

Breed advice: Carol Cooper 01874 712089
Breed rescue: Sue Hislop 01669 650320

Norfolk Terrier

History

Each region bred terriers that were adapted to the local environment, and Norfolk was no exception. The famous Norfolk fens are covered with a network of canals. With the canals came rats - have rats, need terriers. The Norfolk Terrier's ancestors controlled the rat population, and kept them out of barns and stables. They were also used to flush out foxes, and, unlike most other terriers, they were sometimes kept in packs for vermin-hunting.

Two Norfolk Terriers even played their part in canine history. Chris Patten, the former Governor of Hong Kong, became a vocal supporter of pet passports when he had to take his two Norfolks, Whisky and Soda, to France because quarantine regulations prevented him from bringing them from Hong Kong to the UK.

Like this?
Check out these alternatives:

- Australian Terrier
- Border Terrier
- Cairn Terrier
- Norwich Terrier

Character sketch

Being of small stature and highly intelligent, he is easier to control than the larger terriers, but the Norfolk still has the instincts, and will hunt every mole in your garden.

The Norfolk is virtually tireless, and will play with children until utterly exhausted (the children, that is). He likes to have something to do, from snuffling about in leaves under shrubbery to trying to catch rabbits in a field.

As a house dog, he is brilliant and won't drive the neighbours mad with incessant barking. A Norfolk Terrier will love his human family and will be a source of amusement for each individual.

Special considerations
Needs plenty of exercise. Instruct children how to handle him with gentleness and respect. Can be prone to obesity if overfed or fed incorrectly.

Norwich Terriers
Even though they look so alike, the Norwich and the Norfolk Terrier were always separate breeds. The Norwich has prick ears and may have a slightly harsher coat and smaller feet. Norfolks are generally more rounded than their more angular cousins.

Vital statistics

Height:	25 cms
Weight:	4.5-5.5 kgs
Exercise:	●●○○○
Grooming:	●●●○
Noise:	●●○○
Food bill:	£4.50 per week

Country of origin:	Britain
Original function:	Vermin control
Availability:	Difficult

Colours:	Red, wheaten, black and tan, grizzle
Coat type:	Harsh topcoat, with a soft undercoat
Coat care:	Twice-weekly brush and comb. The coat needs stripping every six months, to allow the new coat to grow

Health

Average life span:	14 years
Hereditary disorders:	No problems known to breeders
Hip dysplasia:	Insufficient numbers have been tested

Suitability

Exercise:	As much as the owner can manage. Two or three walks a day would be ideal
Ease of training:	Moderate
Temperament with children:	Very good; children must be trained too, though!
With dogs?	No problems
With cats?	Okay, with his 'own'; will chase other cats
Town or country dog?	Either
Would he happily live in a flat or apartment?	Yes, with adequate exercise
Natural guard dog?	He is protective, and will warn of intruders
Attitude to strangers?	Friendly

Want to know more?

Breed advice: Dorothy Dorkins 01704 568452
Breed rescue: Mrs H Jupp 01327 831097

Character sketch

An independent, brainy and fun dog. Survival of the fittest through some of the coldest climates has, over millennia, produced a dog of extraordinary toughness. They like sleeping out in snow in temperatures below 40°C, their stamina on the hunt is legendary and their scenting powers are exquisite. They have been recorded as picking up the scent of an elk over three miles away and their courage in the face of adversity is renowned.

Their close proximity to man for thousands of years means Elkhounds are particularly fond of human beings and become utterly devoted to their owners.

This lively dog will fit into any home where the family is energetic.

History

Many breeds lay claim to the greatest antiquity, very few however, have the credentials of the Norwegian Elkhound. They come from a group known as the Northern Spitz - dogs distinguished by prick ears, heavy double coats and curly tails. Experts believe that it has, in its origins, the 12,000-year-old dog known as Torvmosehund, *canis familiaris palustris* (swamp hound). Engravings on prehistoric reindeer horn and drawings on cave walls show quite clearly the familiarity between this Spitz type dog and early man.

Four skeletons were found in Western Norway only a few years ago, with bones dating back to between 5 and 4000 years BC. Two skeletons were identified as *canis palustris* and the other two as dogs identical to the Norwegian Elkhound of today.

Like this?
Check out these alternatives:

- Akita
- Alaskan Malamute
- Japanese Shiba Inu
- Keeshond

Special considerations
Take special care of the coat, particularly at moulting time. Make the dog feel he's part of the family.

Vital statistics

Height:	49-52 cms
Weight:	20-23 kgs
Exercise:	●●○○
Grooming:	●●●●
Noise:	●●○○
Food bill:	£7 per week

Country of origin:	Norway
Original function:	Hunting
Availability:	Difficult

Colours:	Dark blue-grey, darker and lighter greys, brindles, yellows, sandy red, red fawns with black points, slight white permissable
Coat type:	Abundant, weather resistant, coarse outer coat, soft, thick undercoat
Coat care:	Weekly brushing, more when moulting

Health

Average life span:	12 years
Hereditary disorders:	Eye-test parents and pups
Hip dysplasia:	13 (breed mean score)

Suitability

Exercise:	These dogs can never have too much! Two miles twice a day will suffice with garden play
Ease of training:	Easily trained
Temperament with children:	First class
With dogs?	Some males can express dominance with other dogs
With cats?	Good
Town or country dog?	Country
Would he happily live in a flat or apartment?	Only with sufficient exercise
Natural guard dog?	Yes
Attitude to strangers?	Quite friendly

Want to know more?

Breed advice: Mrs E Nichols 01530 230313
Breed rescue: Andrew Littlejohn 01563 540194

History

The Old English Sheepdog is a descendent, rather than an ancestor, of the Bearded Collie, and there is no mention of it before the 1800s, which, in dog history terms, makes it middle-aged rather than elderly.

The 'English' bit is probably right, though. The Old English Sheepdog is thought to have originated in the south-west of England with a little help from its Scottish Beardie ancestors and possibly a Russian Owtchar great-great uncle. The 'sheepdog' part is beyond dispute - sturdy, thick-coated dogs were used for the herding, guarding and driving of sheep and cattle.

Character sketch

A boisterous dog, who craves love and affection from his human pack. He exhibits a playful disposition.

The OES is very active and needs plenty of exercise. Being a big dog, it is essential to get control over him from an early age. He is very intelligent and quick to learn, so the trick is to be firm, kind and patient. Make training fun, with a lot of praise, and he will not get bored.

Most people's idea of the OES is garnered from the Dulux television advert, but don't be misled - he doesn't look like that naturally! Maintaining a dog to look like the TV star requires a great deal of work.

As a puppy, no formal exercise is necessary - with the exception of lead-training. Then, when adult, it becomes a different matter. Simply put, the breed is a running machine!

Like this?
Check out these alternatives:

- Bearded Collie
- Bichon Frise
- Briard
- Tibetan Terrier

Special considerations

They need to be kept busy as they can get easily bored and may become destructive.

Vital statistics

Height:	56-61 cms
Weight:	60-80 kgs
Exercise:	●●●●
Grooming:	●●●●
Noise:	●●●○
Food bill:	£7 a week

Country of origin:	England
Original function:	Herding and guarding
Availability:	Easy

Colours:	All shades of grey with white
Coat type:	Thick undercoat with profuse, hard guard hair
Coat care:	Puppies require daily grooming. Adults must be groomed at least twice a week - brushing and combing down to the skin.

Health

Average life span:	10 years
Hereditary disorders:	Eye-test parents and pups
Hip dysplasia:	19 (breed mean score)

Suitability

Exercise:	Play in the garden sufficient for pups. Adults will take as much exercise as you can give - and then some!
Ease of training:	Moderate
Temperament with children:	Very good
With dogs?	Generally good, but some can be dominant
With cats?	Usually okay with the family cat; can be 'iffy' with other cats
Town or country dog?	Either, but prefers the country
Would he happily live in a flat or apartment?	Only with lots of exercise and things to do
Natural guard dog?	Yes
Attitude to strangers?	Watchful

Want to know more?

 Breed advice and rescue: Gill Harwood 01507 588644

History

These elegant little dogs weren't always called Papillons - the French word for butterfly - indeed, they didn't even have their distinctive butterfly-shaped ears to start with.

Now known as Continental Toy Spaniels in most parts of Europe, the Papillon has also been called the Dwarf Spaniel and the Squirrel Dog (because of his bushy tail). To confuse matters further, two varieties of the breed are recognised: the Papillon, which is the most well known in this country; and the Phalene (meaning 'moth'), the older of the two types, which has drop-ears.

Thanks to centuries of close contact with humans, Paps are model companions and have a well-deserved reputation for being playful and affectionate. Some people believe they even have the gift of extra-sensory perception and there are tales of Paps detecting unforeseen dangers or even sensing the presence of ghosts. This may be a tad far-fetched, of course, but Paps are particularly alert and responsive, which is why they make excellent assistance dogs and have been trained very successfully as hearing dogs for deaf people.

Special considerations

He needs nutritious food to maintain his coat and colour. Care must be taken to keep tangles clear from behind the ears.

Like this?
Check out these alternatives:

- Chihuahua
- German Spitz
- Pomeranian
- Löwchen
- Tibetan Spaniel

Character sketch

He may be small, but he likes to rule - the owner must be the leader! This is a happy, amusing and faithful companion, suitable for all ages.

The Papillon is a wonderful companion breed suitable for young and old, living in the country or town. Papillons are 'people dogs' - in fact, they become depressed if kept away from human contact.

Vital statistics

Height:	20-28 cms
Weight:	1-4.5 kgs depending on height
Exercise:	●○○○
Grooming:	●●●○
Noise:	●●○○
Food bill:	£5 per week

Country of origin:	France/Belgium
Original function:	Companion
Availability:	Difficult

Colours:	Black and white, red and white, tri-colour, red sable and white, and lemon and white
Coat type:	Abundant, long, silky and flowing
Coat care:	A light brush and comb daily to keep the coat looking its best

Health

Average life span:	14 years
Hereditary disorders:	Eye-test parents, Von Willebrands disease
Hip dysplasia:	Insufficient numbers have been tested

Suitability

Exercise:	Two or three walks a day, with free-running and games. A fit dog will happily walk for miles
Ease of training:	Fairly easy
Temperament with children:	Outstanding
With dogs?	No problems
With cats?	Okay
Town or country dog?	Either
Would he happily live in a flat or apartment?	Yes
Natural guard dog?	No, but will warn if strangers approach
Attitude to strangers?	Friendly

Want to know more?

Breed advice: Jill Terry 01945 430583
Breed rescue: Debbie Gornall 01772 864585

History

The Jack Russell is one of a handful of dogs that is readily identifiable as a breed but exists outside formal Kennel Club classification. The Parson Russell Terrier is the only variety of these tenacious terriers to hold the correct paperwork for a turn in the Kennel Club show ring.

While Reverend John Russell was an undergraduate in Oxford in 1815, he went for a stroll in the Oxfordshire village of Marston, where a terrier bitch owned by a milkman caught his eye - so he bought the dog, which was probably a Fox Terrier cross of some sort. And so it was that Trump - as the legend has it - became the founder of the Parson Russell Terrier.

He wanted a dog with enough stamina to follow a pack of hounds that was also small enough to go to ground. The Parson Russell Terrier - which is taller than your average Jack Russell - seems more qualified for the former task, which is why it has been described as 'the genuine Jack Russell'.

Like this?
Check out these alternatives:

- Border Terrier
- Irish Terrier
- Norfolk Terrier
- Petit Basset Griffon Vendeen
- Welsh Terrier

Character sketch

A fun dog with a great sense of humour. He is not the easiest dog to train. Being a terrier, he has an independent streak, so patience, kindness and more patience is required. In the home you'll find him a happy-go-lucky, funny, busy, loving dog, who always wants to be by your side.

Special considerations
He must not be allowed off the lead near roads, as he has no understanding of traffic. He can be trained, but needs great patience and lots of fun motivation. He thrives on free-running and play.

Vital statistics

Height:	30-33 cms; Show types 33-36 cms
Weight:	About 6 kgs
Exercise:	●●○○○
Grooming:	●●○○○
Noise:	●●●○
Food bill:	£7 per week for an adult

Country of origin:	Britain
Original function:	Flushing foxes
Availability:	Moderate

Colours:	Predominantly white with black, tan or lemon patches
Coat type:	Smooth, rough or broken-coated
Coat care:	Smooths need a regular brush and polish; roughs and broken-coated dogs are stripped every four to five months

Health

Average life span:	15 years
Hereditary disorders:	Eye-test parents
Hip dysplasia:	Insufficient numbers have been tested

Suitability

Exercise:	It's almost impossible to over-exercise a healthy, adult Russell
Ease of training:	Patience is needed! Be firm, kind but fair
Temperament with children:	Usually good with respectful youngsters, if the dogs are socialised properly
With dogs?	Some males can be dominant with others
With cats?	Okay with own if socialised properly when young; with others, take great care
Town or country dog?	Prefers country life but is adaptable
Would he happily live in a flat or apartment?	Yes, as long as he's exercised sufficiently
Natural guard dog?	Yes, he never misses a sound
Attitude to strangers?	Suspicious initially; friendly after they've been introduced

Want to know more?

Breed advice: Barbara Richards 01736 796656
Breed rescue: Patricia Frost-Copping 01964 615178

History

Legends and myths surrounding the origin of the Pekingese stretch back centuries. Little documentation survives but white Pekes are mentioned in the annals of the Yuan dynasty (1206-1333) and the breed is featured in Chinese art in the Ming dynasty, which began in 1368.

Up to the war between China and the western allies (1856-1860) the Chinese jealously guarded their Pekingese from the west. At the end of the war, five dogs were taken by British officers. The smallest, which weighed 3 lbs, was presented to Queen Victoria, and a picture of this dog was painted and hung in the Royal Academy in 1863.

Like this?
Check out these alternatives:

- Bichon Frise
- Pomeranian
- Pug
- Shih Tzu
- Tibetan Spaniel

Character sketch

The Pekingese has a proud and arrogant carriage and believes he is superior to all other canines. He may be small but he certainly doesn't know this. The breed enjoys more exercise than is commonly supposed, for he is surprisingly active and playful with his family, whom he invariably adores.

Special considerations

These days, the Peke is one of the most popular show dogs. He has been bred to a very high degree of beauty, and while his abundant coat of many colours is his crowning glory, it needs very close maintenance.

Nobody should take on a Pekingese unless they are prepared to maintain the profuse coat, which should be groomed daily. Failure to do so will result in tangling and matting to such an extent as to be uncomfortable, unhygienic and painful.

Vital statistics

Height:	18 cms
Weight:	Not exceeding 5.4 kgs
Exercise:	●○○○
Grooming:	●●●●
Noise:	●○○○
Food bill:	£3.50 per week

Country of origin:	China
Original function:	Companion
Availability:	Moderate
Colours:	All colours and markings except albino and liver
Coat type:	Coarse top coat, thick undercoat, profuse feathering
Coat care:	Daily brush and comb essential to keep the coat tangle free

Health

Average life span:	12 years
Hereditary disorders:	Heart problems
Hip dysplasia:	Insufficient numbers have been tested

Suitability

Exercise:	A daily walk in the park will suffice. Ideally they should have access to a large escape-proof garden
Ease of training:	Very good
Temperament with children:	Very good
With dogs?	Excellent with own breed, may try to dominate others
With cats?	Very good
Town or country dog?	Town
Would he happily live in a flat or apartment?	Yes
Natural guard dog?	Yes
Attitude to strangers?	Friendly

Want to know more?

Breed advice: Eileen Maycock 01252 325880, Sue Addo 01483 876272
Breed rescue: Mrs P Brown 01780 450356

Petit Basset Griffon Vendeen

Like this?
Check out these alternatives:

- Dandie Dinmont Terrier
- Basset Hound
- Beagle
- Dachshund

History

The breeds that may have had a hand in the end product are the Griffon Fauve de Bretagne, Harriers, Dachshunds, and even the Dandie Dinmont Terrier - it's anyone's guess. From this genetic whirlpool emerged two breeds, the Petit and the Grand - little and large!

Character sketch

The PBGV can be a wonderful house dog, integrating completely into family life and loving each member dearly. They will play endlessly with children, providing they are not abused by them.

The breed is said to be naturally clean and is highly intelligent, although their intelligence can lead them into using their own initiative and doing the unexpected. They are trainable with much patience and firm kindness - harsh treatment is counterproductive.

It is safe to say that the breed is not for everyone; they are for people who can understand them and their needs, particularly where exercise and mental stimulation are concerned. It is essential to have a fully fenced area in which they can play without the fear of a great escape.

Special considerations

Despite his melting eyes and gentle aspect, the PBGV is a real hound in all ways. Left to his own devices, he will put his nose down and go. If the scent is strong, he will be deaf to all entreaties, and his owner will not be able to run far or fast enough to catch him. Great care should be taken around livestock - although he will not touch them, his hunting presence may worry them and some farmers are quick on the trigger.

Vital statistics

Height:	33-38 cms
Weight:	11-16 kgs
Exercise:	●●○○○
Grooming:	●●○○○
Noise:	●●○○○
Food bill:	£3.50 per week

Country of origin:	France
Original function:	Hunting
Availability:	Moderate

Colours:	White with lemon or orange; tri-colour or grizzle
Coat type:	Harsh, waterproof outercoat, with a thick undercoat
Coat care:	A weekly groom with a brush and comb will suffice

Health

Average life span:	14 years
Hereditary disorders:	Eye-test parents and pups, epilepsy
Hip dysplasia:	20 (breed mean score)

Suitability

Exercise:	Adult dogs need exercising until you are tired - then take a rest and start again!
Ease of training:	Moderate with patience and kind firmness
Temperament with children:	Very good
With dogs?	Good
With cats?	Okay with 'own' - be careful with others
Town or country dog?	Mainly a country dog
Would he happily live in a flat or apartment?	No
Natural guard dog?	No, but will usually bark at the approach of strangers
Attitude to strangers?	Friendly

Want to know more?

 Breed advice: Vivien Phillips 01442 851225; Linda Lewis 01269 844524; Elaine King 01507 472111
Breed rescue: Rose Phillips 01205 280102

History

Pomerania sounds like a made-up fairytale place full of Cinderella castles and snow queens. It is actually a region of northern Europe on the Baltic coast. Bits of it have historically been in Germany; for a while, some of it was Swedish territory, but most of it is now in Poland.

If that wasn't already complicated enough, the Pomeranian is actually a canine of British construction - his continental cousin is known as the German Dwarf Spitz. But that's not the end of it: in all likelihood, the breed didn't originally come from Pomerania at all, or even Germany. His ancestors were spitz-type dogs - some of the oldest domesticated dogs in the world - who lived in the icy Arctic region and were used for pulling sledges, hunting and house-guarding.

Like this?
Check out these alternatives:

- Chihuahua
- German Spitz
- Japanese Spitz
- Keeshond

Special considerations

One important point: although the Pom is a bright, happy little dog within the family circle, he is a sensitive soul and does not like being left alone. As soon as the door closes, he will object, and it is not unknown for a dog to go into a decline because of loneliness. Indeed, some breeders will not sell a pup unless there is someone at home most of the time, or the company of another dog.

Character sketch

You never own a Pom; he owns you! They are wonderful companion dogs, which is not surprising really, as their bloodlines extend right back to among the first breeds of dog that ever associated with humans - the spitz breeds - so it is built into their nature to be family pets.

Vital statistics

Height:	Usually below 23 cms at shoulder
Weight:	1.8-2.5 kgs
Exercise:	●○○○
Grooming:	●●●●
Noise:	●●●○
Food bill:	£2 per week

Country of origin:	Germany
Original function:	Companion
Availability:	Difficult
Colours:	Whole colours in orange, orange sable, cream and black preferred. There should be no black or white shading
Coat type:	A thick, fluffy undercoat, with a harsh, straight, long outercoat
Coat care:	A deep brush and comb at least once a week

Health

Average life span:	15 years
Hereditary disorders:	Patella luxation, heart problems
Hip dysplasia:	Insufficient numbers have been tested

Suitability

Exercise:	A couple of walks a day, plus play
Ease of training:	As pups, they are easy to train, but they will question the need for obedience when they are older, so start them young!
Temperament with children:	Good, provided the children are trained
With dogs?	Amicable
With cats?	Generally good-tempered
Town or country dog?	Either
Would he happily live in a flat or apartment?	Yes, with exercise and toileting opportunities
Natural guard dog?	Will give a warning bark
Attitude to strangers?	Friendly

Want to know more?

Breed advice: Mrs C Holman 01206 738898
Breed rescue: Mrs Christopher 01686 670387

Portugese Podengo

History

Three dogs of Portuguese origin are now recognised by the Kennel Club - the breed standards for all three of them are described as 'interim' - but these recently recognised breeds are still largely unfamiliar to most of us. Although Portugal was once a European superpower with strong historic links to the UK, most dog watchers in this country would probably find it easier to name dog breeds from far-flung Tibet or Mexico than Portugal.

Different strains of Podengo were developed to reflect habitat and purpose. While the rest of the world might not have noticed, the Podengo family has been quietly thriving as working dogs and companions across Portugal for centuries. The Podengo Grande is now rare, even in its home country, but the little Pequeno - which stands no higher than a school ruler - is starting to get noticed, particularly in the US where it's gathering a reputation as a bright and lively companion.

Special considerations
Portuguese Podengos are not usually greedy eaters. Be sure that the food is nourishing, but a high-protein food should be avoided unless he works or does an enormous amount of exercise.

Character sketch

In the home the Podengo makes a delightful pet; he is frisky and happy right into old age. He has a great fondness for his family and likes to be included in all their activities. The breed is so adaptable to family life that people who own them would never change them for another breed.

Like this?
Check out these alternatives:

- Basenji
- Cairn Terrier
- Miniature Pinscher
- Parson Russell Terrier

Vital statistics

Height:	20-30 cms
Weight:	4-5 kgs
Exercise:	●○○○
Grooming:	●○○○
Noise:	●○○○
Food bill	£4-£5 per week

Country of origin:	Portugal
Original function:	Rabbit hound
Availability:	Moderate

Colours:	All shades of fawn from light to dark. White markings permissible
Coat type:	Smooth or wire
Coat care:	Smooth coats: weekly brush and comb; wires: weekly comb and an occasional handstrip if the hair gets too long

Health

Average life span:	15 years
Hereditary disorders:	None
Hip dysplasia:	Insufficient numbers have been tested

Suitability

Exercise:	A couple of good walks a day, with play in the garden
Ease of training:	Relatively easy, as they want to please
Temperament with children:	Very good; of course, children must be taught to respect him - and all dogs
With dogs?	Excellent
With cats?	Be careful; can be socialised from young to accept the family cat, but his instinct is to hunt small creatures, so be cautious
Town or country dog?	Prefers country life but is adaptable
Would he happily live in a flat or apartment?	If given adequate exercise and mental stimulation
Attitude to strangers?	Initially suspicious, but quickly accepts them if the family does

Want to know more?

 Breed advice and rescue: Betty Judge 01793 783297

Special considerations

This breed thrives on human company. Although relatively easy to train, the Pug is very sensitive and reacts badly to stress, so keep it calm and fun. It's crucial he does not overheat - he must be kept cool in warm weather.

Like this?

Check out these alternatives:

- Boston Terrier
- Cavalier King Charles Spaniel
- Pekingese
- Shih Tzu
- Shar Pei

History

William of Orange brought Pugs to this country when he became King of England in 1689. It was out with the pocket spaniels favoured by the Stuarts, and in with the Pugs. The Pug became immensely fashionable across Europe in the 18th century.

Although the Pug is now considered to be as Dutch as tulips and windmills, it's likely that the breed's origins lie much further east and a lot further back. The Chinese have long favoured flat-faced dogs - possibly due to confusion about what a lion looks like (these great cats are symbolically important, but not actually resident in China). Pug-like dogs are depicted in early Chinese pottery and were kept at court from the 8th century onwards. Pugs, in all likelihood, arrived in Europe with traders of the Dutch East Indian Trading Company in the 1600s - which explains how they were eventually adopted as native Netherlanders.

Character sketch

Easygoing and happy, the Pug is full of fun. He loves children and will play for hours, though children must be taught to be careful around the dog - particularly his eyes.

This breed will happily slot into family life and is intelligent enough to understand what's going on - they very soon know their position. Their comprehension of the family's mood is remarkable and they are masters of easing tensions.

Vital statistics

Height:	Approximately 25-28 cms
Weight:	6-8 kgs
Exercise:	●○○○
Grooming:	●○○○
Noise:	●○○○
Food bill:	£7 per week

Country of origin:	China
Original function:	Companion
Availability:	Moderate

Colours:	Silver, fawn, apricot or black
Coat type:	Fine, smooth, soft and short - feels like velvet
Coat care:	A brush and a comb once a week, followed by a polish with a hound glove is all that's needed

Health

Average life span:	13 years
Hereditary disorders:	Hemivertibrae
Hip dysplasia:	21 (breed mean score)

Suitability

Exercise:	Half an hour a day, with free play, and the dog will be happy
Ease of training:	Fairly straightforward
Temperament with children:	Excellent - but children should treat him carefully and with respect
With dogs?	Good
With cats?	Fine (though cats should be socialised with the dog, too, to prevent eye-scratch injuries)
Town or country dog?	Either
Would he happily live in a flat or apartment?	Yes, with adequate mental and physical exercise
Natural guard dog?	No, he'll probably lick a burglar to death!
Attitude to strangers?	Friendly

Want to know more?

Breed advice: Mrs Gudrun Minton 01685 884487
Breed rescue: John Smith 0114 287 4245; Margaret Trossell 01427 890704

Pyrenean Mountain Dog

History

Pyrenean Mountain Dogs are massive and magnificent - just like the mountain range that is their ancestral home. The Pyrenean's ancestors were mastiff-type dogs with deep roots that can reliably be traced back several thousand years. The Roman writer Varro, who lived in the first century BC, sets out two distinct functions for dogs: hunting game and guarding livestock. The guarding dog he describes is large with hanging ears and, ideally, white - so it can easily be seen.

During the 19th century, the numbers of large predators in the Pyrenees sharply declined, and so large, guarding dogs also went into decline. Fortunately, the breed's fortunes have picked up significantly since then and they have become especially popular in the USA and Japan. Their sheep-guarding days may be drawing to a close, but the qualities that make a good pastoral dog are, happily, the very same qualities that make for a great companion.

Character sketch

The Pyrenean Mountain Dog had to be capable of working without the aid and guidance of humans, and would sometimes be left with a herd for months at a time in the Pyrenees mountains. As a result, the need to make decisions without human intervention has led to a somewhat independent nature in the breed; if they make a decision, there can be no changing their mind.

Special considerations
Puppies shouldn't be over-exercised; training is needed from when young - particularly the 'quiet' command (the breed likes the sound of its own voice!) and the meaning of the word "No".

Like this?
Check out these alternatives:

- Bernese Mountain Dog
- Briard
- Newfoundland
- St Bernard
- Tibetan Mastiff

Vital statistics

Height: Minimum 65-70 cms

Weight: Minimum 40-50 kgs

Exercise: ●●○○

Grooming: ●●●○

Noise: ●●●●

Food bill: £12 per week

Country of origin:	France
Original function:	Protecting sheep and shepherd
Availability:	Variable

Colours:	White, or white with patches of badger, wolf-grey, lemon, orange or tan
Coat type:	Profuse undercoat of long, fine hair; outer coat longer and coarser textured
Coat care:	Thorough, deep grooming is needed at least once a week, more when moulting

Health

Average life span:	10 years
Hereditary disorders:	DNA tests
Hip dysplasia:	12 (breed mean score)

Suitability

Exercise:	As much or as little as you can give for adults - from 40 minutes a day up!
Ease of training:	Basic training is straightforward; advanced training can be difficult
Temperament with children:	Good with respectful children
With dogs?	Generally good, but males can be 'spiky' with each other in the company of females
With cats?	Okay, if socialised with them as puppies
Town or country dog?	Country, but difficult to control off-lead
Would he happily live in a flat or apartment?	Not really, as normal urban activities can result in excessive barking
Natural guard dog?	Yes
Attitude to strangers?	Initially wary

Want to know more?

Breed advice: Briony Lazarides 01458 841782; Mrs J Stannard 01579 348860
Breed rescue: John Shaw 01964 551351

Character sketch

The breed is not for everybody, but for the right person he is a great companion - playful and sometimes even clownish. It must be remembered that he is a fearless hunter and because of that can be dominant, stubborn and has a touch of individualism in his make-up.

History

The word ridgeback contained in the name refers to a ridge of hair growing in the reverse direction to the normal lay of the hair along the backbone. It is a rare phenomenon but also seen in the Hottentot Dog and the Thai Ridgeback. All the ingredients that went into the making of the Rhodesian Ridgeback can only be guessed at. It is almost certain its main forebear is the dog used by the Hottentot tribe of South Africa. Through the years, because of their prowess with the lion hunters the breed was known as the 'Lion Dog' and by 1920 there were many different types as the criteria was not what they looked like but what they could do.

Like this?
Check out these alternatives:

- Anatolian Shepherd Dog
- Great Dane
- Hungarian Vizsla
- Labrador Retriever
- Weimaraner

Special considerations

This is an athletic dog who should not be overfed - a fat Rhodesian Ridgeback is offensive to the eye and unhealthy for the dog. It would be unfair to confine this big, outdoor dog to an apartment. A house in the country with a garden would be ideal so he could enjoy long walks and rambles in the woods as well as games in the garden.

Vital statistics

Height:	61-63 cms
Weight:	29-34 kgs
Exercise:	●●●○
Grooming:	●○○○
Noise:	●○○○
Food bill:	£11 per week

Country of origin:	South Africa
Original function:	Big game hunting
Availability:	Moderate
Colours:	Light to red wheaten. Little white on chest permissable. Dark muzzle and ears accepted
Coat type:	Short, dense, sleek and glossy
Coat care:	Regular brushing to keep the coat at its best

Health

Average life span:	12 years
Hereditary disorders:	Elbow dysplasia, dermold sinus
Hip dysplasia:	11 (breed mean score)

Suitability

Exercise:	Exercise should be restricted to play and lead walking up to the age of six months. Two miles per day afterwards
Ease of training:	Moderate
Temperament with children:	Good
With dogs?	Okay but be aware
With cats?	Okay with his 'own' cats, but watch it with others!
Town or country dog?	Country
Would he happily live in a flat or apartment?	Only with vast amounts of exercise
Natural guard dog?	Yes
Attitude to strangers?	Suspicious

Want to know more?

Breed advice: Mrs Crunden 01303 268305; Peter & Elizabeth Nicholson 01508 482550; Kirsteen Maidment 01280 848701
Breed rescue: Carol and Barrie Davies 020 7485 0691

Rottweiler

○ History

The word 'Rottweiler' - like the word 'Poodle' - is one of those dog names that has become shorthand for a certain set of character traits. The suggestion is that Rottweilers are tenacious, dogged (so to speak) and determined, but perhaps a little aggressive with it. But attempts to portray the Rottweiler as little more than a mindless thug are way off the mark and take no account of the breed's long history as a steadfast and reliable working companion.

The Romans brought these dogs to Europe, alongside their advancing armies. Although they may have looked fierce, it's likely that the dogs' main role was not as soldiers, but as stock managers - armies, after all, need supplies and they travel with large quantities of goods and livestock. The Rottweiler's ancestors probably came about as a result of crosses between these mastiff-type dogs and local German herding dogs.

○ Character sketch

Rottweilers are loving, loyal and great fun. They are intelligent and get easily bored if they have nothing to stimulate their active brain. If you don't give them adequate attention or exercise, they will soon learn to amuse themselves... with dire consequences for your home!

Special considerations

Once full vaccinations are complete, you should take your puppy everywhere dogs are allowed - local shops, outside school gates, puppy training classes, etc. A good place is outside a supermarket where you will find noisy children in pushchairs, squeaky trolleys, and elderly people with walking sticks or in wheelchairs. It cannot be emphasised too strongly that socialising the Rottweiler is paramount.

Like this?
Check out these alternatives:

- Belgian Shepherd Dog
- Dobermann
- Dogue De Bordeaux
- German Shepherd Dog
- Mastiff

○ Vital statistics

Height:	58-69 cms
Weight:	Around 50 kgs
Exercise:	●●●○
Grooming:	●○○○
Noise:	●○○○
Food bill:	Under £10 per week

Country of origin:	Germany
Original function:	Farm dog, security/guard
Availability:	Easy

Colours:	Black with tan markings (from rich tan to mahogany). Any white is undesirable
Coat type:	Coarse, flat top coat. Undercoat is essential on the back and thighs but should not show through the top coat
Coat care:	Occasional brush and a bath if mucky

○ Health

Average life span:	12 years
Hereditary disorders:	Elbow dysplasia, eye-test parents, eye-test pups, dermoid sinus
Hip dysplasia:	12 (breed mean score)

○ Suitability

Exercise:	One to two hours a day, plus garden play
Ease of training:	Easy - this intelligent dog loves to learn
Temperament with children:	Generally good, but no dog, regardless of breed, should ever be left unsupervised with a child
With dogs?	Good, provided they are well socialised
With cats?	Usually good, provided he's been raised with them and introduced carefully
Town or country dog?	Prefers the country
Would he happily live in a flat or apartment?	Not really, unless it was a large garden flat
Natural guard dog?	Yes, very much so
Attitude to strangers?	Suspicious

Want to know more?

Breed advice: Dave & Roni Parish 020 8393 3771; Kimberley McDonald 01793 324466; Tracy St Clair Pearce 01206 272736
Breed rescue: The Rottweiler Rescue Trust, Peter Beach 01689 855334

Character sketch

They are gentle, affectionate and intelligent. They can be a little standoffish with strangers, but once a friend, always a friend. They are sociable with adults and children and get on well with other animals.

They are an easy breed to train in basic obedience, as they are quick to learn, especially as they love their special titbits. Work out your house rules from the beginning! They are not a particularly noisy breed, but will let you know when somebody is around.

Special considerations

The Rough Collie's hearing is very sensitive, which means fireworks and thunder can be a problem. Desensitising CDs that you play to your puppies are very helpful.

Like this?

Check out these alternatives:

- Anatolian Shepherd Dog
- Bearded Collie
- Belgian Shepherd Dog
- Border Collie
- Borzoi

History

Practically everyone knows a 'Lassie dog' when they see one, but how many people realise that the breed is more properly known as the Rough Collie? After all, 'rough' isn't exactly the first word that springs to mind when you see one of these glamorous canines.

For many generations, the collie remained a farmer's dog that was rarely seen in the parlours or pantries of the metropolitan set. With the dawn of the dog beauty show, however, all that was to change.

Queen Victoria is generally credited with having brought the Rough Collie out of Highland obscurity and into the urban spotlight. This is not, of course, surprising: Victoria was responsible for popularising lots of dog breeds that had previously been little known to the general British public.

Vital statistics

Height:	51-61 cms
Weight:	Approximately 20-22 kgs
Exercise:	●●●○
Grooming:	●●●●
Noise:	●●○○
Food bill:	£8 per week

Country of origin:	UK
Original function:	Working sheepdog
Availability:	Fairly easy

Colours:	Sable and white; tri-coloured; blue merle; sable (any shade of gold)
Coat type:	The outside coat is coarse, very dense and straight. The undercoat is thick, soft and abundant.
Coat care:	A thorough daily brush

Health

Average life span:	12 years
Hereditary disorders:	Eye-test parents and pups, DNA tests available for gray collie syndrome and Ivermectin sensitivity
Hip dysplasia:	12 (breed mean score)

Suitability

Exercise:	At least one hour a day
Ease of training:	Straightforward
Temperament with children:	Very good, though no dog (of any breed) should be left alone with infants
With dogs?	No problems
With cats?	Will usually chase, but is okay with his 'own' cats if socialised from when young
Town or country dog?	Prefers country
Would he happily live in a flat or apartment?	Not ideal. Depends on the size and if there's access to a garden
Natural guard dog?	No, but will warn if strangers approach
Attitude to strangers?	Usually friendly

Want to know more?

Breed advice: Mrs G Lancaster 01494 713406; Sharon Gladwell 01736 756043; Chantal Scott 01673 857541
Breed Rescue: Mr J Tait 01904 636164

Samoyed

History

The Samoyed is part of the spitz family - one of the most ancient of all the dog groups - and is related to the huskies of Greenland and Alaska. Spitz-type dogs have been kept for thousands of years by the indigenous peoples of the Arctic region.

Many of the Samoyeds now in the west have ancestors that were once used by polar explorers. Other Samoyeds came to the west via royal connections. The tsars of Russia were impressed by these splendid creatures from the frozen north and gave them as gifts to other European royals.

There are still Samoyed-like dogs working with the tribal peoples of northern Siberia, but these traditionally nomadic dogs have also migrated to countless homes across the world, where they are enjoying life as equally valued companions.

Character sketch

A happy, laughing dog, full of goodwill to humans. A good all-round pet dog in the right hands.

Special considerations

It is important to consider the coat of a Samoyed, as there is a lot of grooming involved. They have a double coat, consisting of a short, soft undercoat and a longer, harsh outer coat. A good pin brush and comb will be needed to keep a Sam looking nice, and grooming will also keep the coat clean. Puppies should be groomed for five to 10 minutes a day to get them accustomed to the procedure, as there is going to be a lot of coat to contend with when the pup is fully grown.

Like this?
Check out these alternatives:

- Bichon Frise
- German Spitz
- Japanese Spitz
- Schipperke
- Tibetan Spaniel

Vital statistics

Height:	46-56 cms
Weight:	18-30 kgs
Exercise:	●●●○
Grooming:	●●●●
Noise:	●●●○
Food bill:	£7 per week

Country of origin:	Siberia
Original function:	Herding and sledding
Availability:	Moderately easy

Colours:	Pure white, white with cream or biscuit. The outer coat is silver tipped
Coat type:	Thick, close, short undercoat, with harsh but not wiry guard hairs growing through
Coat care:	Daily brushing and a thorough comb through once a week

Health

Average life span:	13 years
Hereditary disorders:	Eye-test parents, heart problems. DNA test available for eye problems
Hip dysplasia:	13 (breed mean score)

Suitability

Exercise:	At least an hour a day with free running
Ease of training:	Have an independent streak, but are usually highly motivated by food, so training is possible
Temperament with children:	Super, but do make sure children treat him with the same respect!
With dogs?	Great
With cats?	Good, if socialised when young
Town or country dog?	Prefers the country but is adaptable
Would he happily live in a flat or apartment?	Not recommended
Natural guard dog?	No, but will warn of anything unusual
Attitude to strangers?	Loves people full-stop

Want to know more?

Breed advice: Gina Hounslow 0161 217 9008
Breed rescue: Brenda Walker 0115 928 1856

Like this?
Check out these alternatives:

- Belgian Shepherd Dog
- German Spitz
- Japanese Spitz
- Samoyed

Character sketch

If you like a super-active dog who enjoys shoving his sharp little nose into all your business, this is the breed for you. If Schipperkes have a fault it is that they are noisy; their penetrative bark is an irritation to neighbours, but they can be taught to be quiet. They are wonderful guard dogs and very little will get past them; they seem to sleep with one eye open. They don't seem to realise that they are small; if they perceive a threat from another dog, they'll stand up for themselves fearlessly.

Special considerations

If left alone for long, this breed will find things to do that may be contrary to your liking! This is a 'big dog in a small package' - more suited to those who have owned large working or pastoral breeds before.

History

While many believe the breed belongs firmly in the spitz family, it has been suggested that this classification results from confusion with the Dutch Keeshond and that the Schipperke is, in fact, a small version of the Belgian Shepherd Dog.

The breed's name should give us a clue. 'Schipper' is the Flemish word for skipper, and 'ke' is a diminutive: so the dog's name means 'little skipper' - which seems appropriate for a barge dog. However, some people feel this name is inauthentic and that the name is actually derived from the Flemish word 'scheper', which means shepherd.

Vital statistics

Height:	30-35 cms
Weight:	5.5-7.5 kgs
Exercise:	●●○○
Grooming:	●●○○
Noise:	●●○○
Food bill:	£5 per week

Country of origin:	Belgium
Original function:	Guard dogs and ratters on barges
Availability:	Not easy

Colours:	Mostly black, but other whole colours are permitted
Coat type:	Abundant, dense and harsh. Smooth on head, legs and ears, with a thick mane
Coat care:	Brush twice a week unless moulting, then every day. Sheds twice a year

Health

Average life span:	14 years
Hereditary disorders:	None
Hip dysplasia:	Insufficient numbers have been tested

Suitability

Exercise:	At least a half-hour walk, twice per day, when adult, plus quality play
Ease of training:	Varies. They are independent-minded but like to play games and are toy-oriented
Temperament with children:	Excellent, though children should be taught to be respectful
With dogs?	Good; males can be dominant sometimes
With cats?	Good, if brought up with them; likely to chase any neighbourhood cats!
Town or country dog?	Country
Would he happily live in a flat or apartment?	Yes, if adequately stimulated
Natural guard dog?	Yes
Attitude to strangers?	Suspicious

Want to know more?

Breed advice: Mrs Boles 01283 212108
Breed rescue: Lesley Thorne 0161 799 4251

Scottish Terrier

History

At one time, any dog that was used in Scotland to go to ground was called a Scottish or Scotch Terrier, particularly when shown in England. During the early days of formal dog shows, there was much confusion and often heated debate about the finer points of the breeds that would eventually become known as the Cairn, the Skye and the Scottish Terriers.

Today, the Scottish Terrier is easily identifiable by anyone with even a passing knowledge of dogs and they are still often used as a motif on all sorts of things from handbags to knitwear. Yet their numbers have declined sharply in recent years. Still, the Scottie's not ready for retirement yet - the dog that left the Highlands and found friends across the world has too many admirers for that.

Character sketch

This is a little dog with a huge personality. For those looking for the adoring, tail-wagging, can't-live-without-you type dog, then get a Labrador! Scotties are far too feisty and independent for that type of behaviour and live life on their own terms. They can be affectionate, playful and adorable when they want, yet prepare yourself for periods when they are too busy doing their own important Scottie thing to wag their tail for you.

Like this?
Check out these alternatives:

- Irish Terrier
- Welsh Terrier
- West Highland White Terrier
- Cairn Terrier
- Fell Terrier

Special considerations
This highly intelligent breed needs lots of mental stimulation in the form of training, games etc. Gain his respect with firm, kind training - shouting will make him switch off!

Vital statistics

Height:	15.5-28 cms
Weight:	8.5-10.5 kgs
Exercise:	●●○○
Grooming:	●●●●
Noise:	●○○○
Food bill:	£4 per week

Country of origin:	Scotland
Original function:	Vermin control
Availability:	Not easy

Colours:	Black, brindle or wheaten
Coat type:	A thick, soft undercoat, with a thick, wiry, weather-resistant topcoat
Coat care:	A thorough brush through at least once a week. Needs professional grooming for the show ring

Health

Average life span:	12 years
Hereditary disorders:	Patella luxation, Von Willebrands disease - DNA test available
Hip dysplasia:	Insufficient numbers have been tested

Suitability

Exercise:	As much or as little as you can give
Ease of training:	Okay, with patience and kindness
Temperament with children:	Playful and loving with respectful children
With dogs?	Non-aggressive. However, although the Scottie will not seek an altercation, he won't back down if under threat
With cats?	Okay with 'own'; watch it with others!
Town or country dog?	Either
Would he happily live in a flat or apartment?	Yes, providing he's adequately exercised and stimulated
Natural guard dog?	A great watchdog
Attitude to strangers?	Friendly

Want to know more?

Breed advice & rescue: Mrs Tovey 01664 813179

History

It has been said that the Shar-Pei can win the heart of a hermit and the love of a dog hater. Nevertheless, despite this glowing recommendation, the Shar-Pei was recorded as the rarest breed of dog in the world by the *Guinness Book of Records* until the late 1970s.

It seems likely, though, that the Shar-Pei started life in Southern China and was used as an all-purpose guarding, herding and hunting dog by peasant farmers. The dog with a 'warrior scowl' was also used for fighting. The Shar-Pei lost favour as a fighting breed, however, when larger, more ferocious Mastiff-type dogs were imported into the country. The dog continued to help out around the farm, however, and is still a working dog in some areas of China today.

Like this?
Check out these alternatives:

- Boxer
- Dogue De Bordeaux
- Pug
- Bulldog

Character sketch

A happy family dog, the Shar-Pei is very playful. Highly intelligent, he can appear aloof, but enjoys nothing more than being involved in all family activities. A feature of the breed is their fondness of children, whom they are happy to be with and guard all day.

Special considerations
Be careful to buy from a responsible breeder who exhibits his dogs because he is likely to produce puppies to the breed standard, which calls for no excessive skin on the body and condemns utterly the conditions that cause eye problems. Puppy buyers are well advised to ask to see the mother of the puppy and to satisfy themselves that the litter has been well socialised, preferably by being reared in the house.

Vital statistics

Height:	46-51 cms
Weight:	18-20 kgs
Exercise:	●●○○
Grooming:	●●●○
Noise:	●●○○
Food bill:	£7 per week

Country of origin:	China
Original function:	Hunting, guarding and herding
Availability:	Moderate
Colours:	Any solid colour
Coat type:	Short, bristly and harsh to the touch. Stands off from the body, and is flatter on the limbs
Coat care:	A quick brush with a rubber mitt once a week

Health

Average life span:	11 years
Hereditary disorders:	None
Hip dysplasia:	17 (breed mean score)

Suitability

Exercise:	These dogs will take as much, or as little exercise, as you want to give
Ease of training:	Straightforward - this is an intelligent breed
Temperament with children:	Outstanding
With dogs?	Good
With cats?	Okay with his own; with others, be careful!
Town or country dog?	Either
Would he happily live in a flat or apartment?	Yes, with adequate exercise
Natural guard dog?	Yes
Attitude to strangers?	Aloof

Want to know more?

Breed advice & rescue: Jennie Baker 01945 410787

○ Character sketch

Small, affectionate, intelligent and trainable, the Shih Tzu makes a super pet. They don't need a huge amount of exercise but are energetic, sociable dogs, and can be trained to walk fair distances despite their short legs. Beware though - they do have an independent streak!

Special considerations

Children need to be taught to handle them gently, as the breed has protruding eyes which are easily injured. Do not overfeed - they easily become overweight.

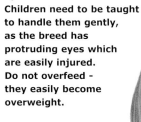

○ History

The Shih Tzu's ancestors came originally from Tibet, where small dogs resembling today's Lhasa Apsos and Tibetan Terriers were kept by monks as companions and bed-warmers! They were sometimes given as gifts, which is how they ended up in China, and it's thought the Shih Tzu is probably the result of a cross between Tibetan Apsos and Chinese Pekingese, although nobody knows for sure.

Shih Tzu were virtually unknown in the west until the beginning of the 20th century. They were originally shown alongside Lhasa Apsos until they were recognised as a distinct breed in the 1930s. They soon became immensely popular, and the Queen's father, King George VI, owned one called Choo-Choo. At the end of the Second World War, many American servicemen returned from the eastern front with a Shih Tzu for their wife or mother, and the breed is still one of America's favourites, as well as being very popular in this country.

Like this?
Check out these alternatives:

- Havanese
- Maltese
- Tibetan Terrier
- Pekingese
- Tibetan Spaniel

○ Vital statistics

Height:	No more than 27 cms
Weight:	4.5-8 kgs
Exercise:	●○○○
Grooming:	●●●○
Noise:	●○○○
Food bill:	£5 per week

Country of origin:	China/Tibet
Original function:	Companion
Availability:	Easy

Colours:	All colours and combinations of colours are acceptable
Coat type:	Long, dense and straight topcoat with a good undercoat
Coat care:	A daily brush and comb is essential to keep the coat looking its best

○ Health

Average life span:	14 years
Hereditary disorders:	None known to breeders
Hip dysplasia:	Insufficient numbers have been tested

○ Suitability

Exercise:	Ideally two 20-minute walks a day. They love to spend time on the sofa
Ease of training:	Average
Temperament with children:	Good
With dogs?	No problems
With cats?	Usually no problems as long as carefully introduced
Town or country dog?	Town
Would he happily live in a flat or apartment?	Yes
Natural guard dog?	No
Attitude to strangers?	Friendly

Want to know more?

Breed advice: Mrs Pat Gregory 01666 822380
Breed rescue: Sue Hills 01702 203444; Pauline Read 01923 675069; Mrs Joyce Ellis 01795 474416

History

The St Bernard gets its name from St Bernard de Menthon, who preached the gospel in the Alps region until his death in 1008. He founded a monastery and hospice at the highest point of the Great St Bernard Pass, one of the most ancient routes through the Alps. The hospice offered a warm welcome to the weary traveller. All true - but there is no evidence to suggest that dogs played an integral role in the daily life of the hospice in the Middle Ages. By the 18th century, though, we start to get accounts of lost travellers found and saved by these courageous dogs, and the legend of the Good Samaritan Dog was born. There is probably an element of truth in that the monks did rely on their dogs to guide them through the snow, and some people would certainly have perished if the dogs had not located them.

Like this?
Check out these alternatives:

- Leonberger
- Newfoundland
- Tibetan Mastiff
- Pyrenean Mountain Dog

Character sketch

A big softie who loves human company, and will draw attention wherever he goes. He will follow you round the house like a shadow. If you're at all house-proud, though, don't get a St Bernard - that slobber gets everywhere.

Special considerations
Be careful not to over-exercise dogs under a year old. Be aware that bloat can occur in the breed - watch for any signs of stomach swelling or discomfort and seek immediate veterinary advice.

Vital statistics

Height:	Minimum 70-75 cms
Weight:	Can weigh over 60 kgs
Exercise:	●●○○
Grooming:	●●●●
Noise:	●●○○
Food bill:	£10 per week

Country of origin:	Switzerland
Original function:	Avalanche search and rescue
Availability:	Fairly easy

Colours:	Orange, mahogany brindle, red brindle. Some white permitted on muzzle, blaze on the face, forelegs, collar, chest, tail tip
Coat type:	Two types of coat: rough and smooth
Coat care:	Brush and comb through at least once a week

Health

Average life span:	8½ years
Hereditary disorders:	Elbow dysplasia; some heart problems
Hip dysplasia:	21 (breed mean score)

Suitability

Exercise:	When young, play in the garden and a gentle stroll will suffice. From a year old, slowly build up to longer distances
Ease of training:	Straightforward
Temperament with children:	Very good, though he can be clumsy so careful supervision is required
With dogs?	Friendly
With cats?	Usually fine if brought up with them
Town or country dog?	Prefers country life but is adaptable, provided his needs are met
Would he happily live in a flat or apartment?	Generally they are just too big for it to be successful
Natural guard dog?	Yes
Attitude to strangers?	Friendly

Want to know more?

Breed advice: Miss P H Muggleton 01773 872535; Diane Deuchar Fawcett 01723 584696; Briony Lazarides 01458 841782
Breed rescue: Mrs Liz Derrins 01333 312068

Staffordshire Bull Terrier

History

Bull-, bear- and badger-baiting were popular pastimes in medieval times, and dogs were bred to take part in this so-called sport. Originally big, rough dogs were used but slowly realisation dawned that a more lithe dog was needed, which could more easily evade the bulls' horns, and the beginnings of the Bulldog began to appear. Dogfights were also public entertainment, and in the mid 1700s the Duke of Hamilton was given the dubious title of "father of the modern fighting dog" for his breed lines. From paintings, experts can detect a likeness between his dogs and modern Staffords.

In the early 1800s a Colonel McNeil was sent to Ireland, where he became friendly with the Lord of Kerry, who kept Irish Wolfhounds. He gave McNeill his famous fighting dog, a blue bitch, which McNeill bred to one of the Duke of Hamilton's Bull Terriers, and many believe that American Pit Bull Terriers, American Stafford Terriers and our own Staffords have inherited these genes.

A breed club was formed in 1935, the name coming from the county where most were bred.

Like this?
Check out these alternatives:

- Bull Terrier
- Bulldog
- Boston Terrier

Character sketch

A dog with a sense of humour, who makes a devoted family friend. Keep children in the family under control - an excitable child equals an excitable Stafford.

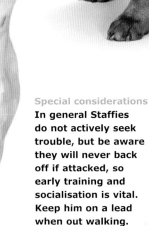

Special considerations

In general Staffies do not actively seek trouble, but be aware they will never back off if attacked, so early training and socialisation is vital. Keep him on a lead when out walking.

Vital statistics

Height:	36-41 cms
Weight:	11-17 kgs
Exercise:	●●●○
Grooming:	●○○○
Noise:	●●●○
Food bill:	£5 per week

Country of origin:	Britain
Original function:	Canine gladiators; now pets and show dogs
Availability:	Easy
Colours:	Brindle, black, fawn, red and white, or any of the solid colours with white
Coat type:	Short and smooth
Coat care:	Brush over once a week with a hound glove

Health

Average life span:	12 years
Hereditary disorders:	Parents and pups should be eye-tested. Both parents should be DNA tested for a neurometabolic disorder
Hip dysplasia:	13 (breed mean score)

Suitability

Exercise:	Do not over-exercise when young, enjoys lots of exercise when fully grown
Ease of training:	Easy, if reward-based and short spells
Temperament with children:	Very good
With dogs?	Be very careful at all times
With cats?	Usually okay with 'own', will chase others
Town or country dog?	Either, but probably prefers the country
Would he happily live in a flat or apartment?	Yes
Natural guard dog?	No, too friendly and trusting
Attitude to strangers?	Watchful

Want to know more?

Breed advice: Jo Toms 01963 23054; Jamie Mace 01243 821672; Mrs Mclaunchlan 01642 783948

Breed rescue: Bob Whittall 01539 530245; John and Gwen Laker 01227 471674

History

All three sizes of Schnauzer (Standard, Giant and Miniature) trace their roots back to southern Germany. By the 1880s, breed standards were beginning to be established. In the early days of the dog show, Schnauzers were lumped together with Pinschers (the German word for 'terrier'), but at an international show in 1897 a dog named Schnauzer won the wire-haired Pinscher class, and this dog's name was chosen when the Schnauzer was recognised as a separate breed.

Schnauzer-type dogs, though, with the distinctive facial fuzz, were used to guard homes and farms in 15th century Europe, and the artist Durer immortalised his own pet Schnauzer in several paintings around the 1490s. The Standard Schnauzer has today lost ground to his Miniature friend, but is still popular in many parts of Europe.

Like this?
Check out these alternatives:

- Miniature Schnauzer
- Irish Terrier
- Dobermann

Special considerations
Proper and consistent training is vital from the beginning. This is not a breed for the first-time owner. Breeders' stock should be checked for temperament.

Character sketch

If you know how to train and treat your Schnauzer, he is a fantastically loyal family dog, forever guarding his family. That said, he is self-willed and strong, and can be wary of strangers. He makes a great guard dog - which means he barks! He has enormous energy, and ideally once fully grown needs regular long walks as well as mental stimulation. Schnauzers can be stubborn, and will get bored repeating the same exercise again and again, so keep training sessions short and varied.

Vital statistics

Height:	45.5-48 cms
Weight:	17-18 kgs
Exercise:	●●●○
Grooming:	●●●●
Noise:	●●○○
Food bill:	£8 per week

Country of origin:	Germany
Original function:	Farm dog, watch dog and guard
Availability:	Moderate

Colours:	Solid black, or pepper and salt
Coat type:	Extremely harsh and straight, with a heavy undercoat
Coat care:	A weekly brush and comb; keep the beard clean. A show dog needs to be handstripped; pets can be clipped

Health

Average life span:	14 years
Hereditary disorders:	Heart problems
Hip dysplasia:	23 (breed mean score)

Suitability

Exercise:	Will take as much exercise as you can give
Ease of training:	The Schnauzer learns quickly, but needs early training and socialisation
Temperament with children:	Can be "iffy" unless he is properly and consistently trained
With dogs?	Generally okay - again, must be socialised and trained
With cats?	Be watchful
Town or country dog?	Flexible - but needs regular exercise
Would he happily live in a flat or apartment?	Yes, if given adequate mental and physical stimulation
Natural guard dog?	Yes
Attitude to strangers?	Suspicious initially

Want to know more?

Breed advice: Karen Carroll 01524 411220
Breed rescue: Hilary Lockyer 01992 892256

Swedish Vallhund

History

There was more to the Vikings than marauding and plundering. They also did perfectly peaceable things, like farming. Farmers have long appreciated the value of a hard-working canine, and the Swedish Vallhund's ancestors probably lived alongside these early Scandinavian people. Sometimes known as the Vikingarnas Dog, or the Little Cattle Dog of the Vikings, the Vallhund is an ancient breed that has been herding cattle in his homeland for centuries. He was also kept as an all-purpose farm dog, with vermin control and guarding duties.

The Swedish Vallhund is very similar to the Welsh Corgi. We know the Vikings settled in small numbers in Pembrokeshire, but we don't know if they brought dogs with them, or took a shine to the dogs they found in Wales and took some home. We'll probably never know which came first, the Corgi or the Vallhund, but it seems safe to assume there is a family connection.

The breed was not introduced to the UK until 1973, and received official Kennel Club recognition in 1980, but remains rare outside Sweden.

Like this?
Check out these alternatives:

- Australian Cattle Dog
- Corgi
- German Spitz
- Norwegian Elkhound

Character sketch

An adaptable dog with a happy disposition, the Swedish Vallhund always looks as if he is smiling. He makes a lively and affectionate companion. They don't require huge amounts of grooming or exercise - though they will happily accompany you for miles if you wish.

Special considerations

This breed likes his food, so watch his weight and ensure he remains slim. He can be an annoying barker - if allowed! He will moult twice a year, and you will find hair everywhere during this time.

Vital statistics

Height:	31-35 cms
Weight:	11.5-16 kgs
Exercise:	●●○○
Grooming:	●○○○
Noise:	●●●○
Food bill:	£6 per week

Country of origin:	Sweden
Original function:	Cattle dog
Availability:	Not easy

Colours:	Various shades of grey sable or red
Coat type:	Medium length, close and harsh, with a thick, soft undercoat
Coat care:	Needs a thorough brush and comb once a week; three times a week when moulting (twice a year - heavily!)

Health

Average life span:	12 years
Hereditary disorders:	Parents should be eye-tested, patella luxation
Hip dysplasia:	12 (breed mean score)

Suitability

Exercise:	A minimum of two 20-minute walks a day
Ease of training:	These intelligent dogs can be a little stubborn, but they are very trainable
Temperament with children:	Very good
With dogs?	Affable unless confronted
With cats?	Usually good, but be careful
Town or country dog?	Either
Would he happily live in a flat or apartment?	Yes, with the right physical and mental stimulation
Natural guard dog?	Good watchdog; no sound goes unnoticed
Attitude to strangers?	Friendly

Want to know more?

Breed advice: Jacqui Bayliss 01795 881331
Breed rescue: Vicky Allsop 01295 253012

Special considerations
The Tibetan Mastiff is a large dog, who demands respect. Kind patience is needed in training to achieve success. This breed likes peace and quiet, and needs space.

Like this?
Check out these alternatives:

- Bernese Mountain Dog
- Mastiff
- Newfoundland
- Pyrenean Mastiff

History

There were Mastiff-type dogs in England 2,000 years ago, and similar breeds were depicted and described in the far and near east at least a thousand years before that. Mastiff-type dogs often make an appearance in art and artefacts from ancient Greece. It is theoretically possible that all these dogs were descended from ancient Tibetan stock, which was transported by Central Asian nomads, but there is no concrete evidence.

The Tibetan Mastiff had been guarding livestock in Tibet for possibly as long as there had been livestock to guard. But these previously unknown dogs made an impression on the handful of brave - or foolhardy - western travellers who began arriving in the treacherous Himalayan region during the 19th century. Inevitably, some of these dogs were taken home as objects of curiosity, fascination and delight.

Character sketch

A magnificent guard dog who takes his responsibilities seriously. He has an aloof quality but loves his family and can be stubborn, though persistent training will bring dividends. They are calm and well behaved around the house.

The adult dog needs to be well exercised daily. As with other giant breeds, Tibetan Mastiffs do not need a lot of exercise for the first year, so short walks and play in the garden will prove enough to start with. Food should not be a problem, as Tibetan Mastiffs are not known to be fussy eaters.

Vital statistics

Height:	61-66 cms and over
Weight:	57-63.5 kgs; some are heavier
Exercise:	●●●○
Grooming:	●●●○
Noise:	●○○○
Food bill:	£10 per week

Country of origin:	Tibet
Original function:	Guard, livestock guard and watchdog
Availability:	Not easy

Colours:	Black, black and tan, gold, grey and blue. Minimal white markings are acceptable. Tan markings around eyes, on chest, lower leg and under tail are permissible
Coat type:	Heavy-coated. The outercoat is straight and thick; the undercoat is also thick
Coat care:	Daily brush and comb

Health

Average life span:	12 years
Hereditary disorders:	No problems known to breeders
Hip dysplasia:	14 (breed mean score)

Suitability

Exercise:	Play and short walks when a pup, slowly increasing to a formidable amount when fully-grown
Ease of training:	If you ask nicely, will probably co-operate; 'tell' him, and he's likely to ignore you!
Temperament with children:	Very good, but children must be taught to respect him
With dogs?	Generally good; inter-male aggression can occur
With cats?	Be careful
Town or country dog?	Prefers country life
Would he happily live in a flat or apartment?	Yes, if sufficiently exercised
Natural guard dog?	Very much so
Attitude to strangers?	Initially suspicious

Want to know more?

 Breed advice & rescue: Mrs P Jeans-Brown 0121 779 2692

Tibetan Spaniel

History

Some experts believe that because of the Tibetan Spaniel's incredible far-sightedness, they were developed to sit in the towers of monasteries to warn of the approach of strangers. The breed may have been the origin of the Pekingese and Japanese Chin. Some theories state that the Chinese sent Pekingese to Tibet, which were then mated with the Lhasa Apso to produce the Tibetan Spaniel.

Back in the 1930s, they were bred by the Dalai Lama. Buddhism prohibits the killing of animals and dogs were allowed to roam unhindered. Sadly, the occupying Chinese army operated a campaign to exterminate all dogs. Happily, they did not succeed and specimens of Tibetan breeds can still be found.

Tibetan dog breeds were virtually unknown in Britain until the Younghusband Expeditionary Force entered the country and a few dogs returned with soldiers. The famous artist Maude Earl depicted Tibetan Spaniels in a painting around 1898.

Like this?
Check out these alternatives:

- Cavalier King Charles Spaniel
- King Charles Spaniel
- Pekingese
- Shih Tzu

Character sketch

An outgoing, entertaining companion, the Tibetan Spaniel is alert and very loyal, but has a strong independent streak. They are innately intelligent, and it was noted upon their arrival in Britain that the adults learnt English very quickly. He also has an elephantine memory; it is said they never forget a friend and never forgive an enemy.

They don't need a tremendous amount of exercise, but they do have boundless energy. They are warm-hearted, affectionate and enjoy being part of family activities.

Special considerations
An escapologist, the Tibetan Spaniel needs a dog-proof garden. He is very inquisitive and must be kept on a lead in traffic areas.

Vital statistics

Height:	Approx 25 cms
Weight:	4-7 kgs
Exercise:	●●○○○
Grooming:	●●○○○
Noise:	●●○○○
Food bill:	£5 per week

Country of origin:	Tibet
Original function:	Watchdog and companion
Availability:	Fairly difficult

Colours:	All colours and mixes. Gold and silver sable are the most popular
Coat type:	Double-coated, with a silky top coat. The legs, tails and ears should be well feathered
Coat care:	A weekly brush and comb

Health

Average life span:	14½ years
Hereditary disorders:	Eye-test parents
Hip dysplasia:	12 (breed mean score)

Suitability

Exercise:	Plenty of exercise, especially free running. Best exercised on an extending lead due to deafness when it is time to go home!
Ease of training:	Easy, but can be strong-willed
Temperament with children:	Good - provided children are respectful
With dogs?	Good with own breed, but can be dominant
With cats?	Very good with his own cats; not too bad with others
Town or country dog?	Okay with both
Would he happily live in a flat or apartment?	Yes, with exercise
Natural guard dog?	Makes a good watchdog
Attitude to strangers?	Suspicious

Want to know more?

Breed advice: Miss B E Croucher 01792 470417; Pauline Lock 01666 510859; Connie Rankin 01896 823642

Breed rescue: Miss B E Croucher 01792 470417

Character sketch

An extremely happy breed, the Tibetan Terrier is a great house dog. He's lively and mischievous well into old age, so is great fun to have around.

Also, Tibetans are intelligent and will learn quickly, but, having learnt something, they will suddenly become forgetful. For example, after correctly retrieving a ball half a dozen times, a Tibetan will forget on the seventh time and run away, wondering why you don't fetch your own ball!

Recall training is essential and the Tibetan likes his food, so watch his weight.

Special considerations

Make sure he has shade and plenty of clean water on very hot days. Training classes are essential: Tibetans can be pig-headed. Be patient and kind when training.

Like this?

Check out these alternatives:

- Bearded Collie
- Briard
- Havanese

History

Known as 'holy dogs' or 'luck bringers', the legend goes that Tibetan Terriers come from Tibet's mysterious Lost Valley. It is also said that the dogs were kept by Buddhist monks in the monasteries of Tibet. They were associated with good luck and never sold, but sometimes given as gifts to travellers.

Still an unusual breed in this country, the Tibetan Terrier might have escaped our attention completely if it hadn't been for Agnes Greig, a British doctor who worked in India during the 1920s. A Tibetan man gave Dr Greig a puppy as a gesture of gratitude for successfully operating on his wife. Dr Greig had an interest in dogs and soon acquired a mate for her luck bringer. When she returned to the UK, the doctor brought her dogs and set about establishing the breed.

Vital statistics

Height:	36-41 cms
Weight:	Approx 9-11.5 kgs
Exercise:	●○○○
Grooming:	●●●○
Noise:	●○○○
Food bill:	£6 per week

Country of origin:	Tibet
Original function:	Farm dog
Availability:	Moderate

Colours:	All colours except liver and chocolate
Coat type:	Top coat is like human hair in texture. It should be straight, though it can be wavy (not curly)
Coat care:	A thorough brush and comb is needed at least every other day

Health

Average life span:	14 years
Hereditary disorders:	Eye-test parents, deafness
Hip dysplasia:	14 (breed mean score)

Suitability

Exercise:	Happy with play in the garden and two daily walks, or long, country hikes
Ease of training:	Stubborn streak can make training a little challenging, but patience will pay off
Temperament with children:	Super, provided they are respected by youngsters
With dogs?	Good
With cats?	Very likely to chase, but can be trained when young to accept the family's cats
Town or country dog?	Either
Would he happily live in a flat or apartment?	With sufficient exercise
Natural guard dog?	No, but will warn if strangers approach
Attitude to strangers?	Initially suspicious, but soon friendly

Want to know more?

Breed advice: Avril Mclean 01560 482527; Krista Guziolek 01544 231839; Pat Noujaim 01296 437050

Breed rescue: No known breed rescue

History

The Weimaraner's first recognisable origin was in the state of Weimar, Germany - the Grand Prince Karl August came across the breed while hunting around 1787.

The story of how Weimaraners came to Britain has a romantic element. In Berlin, two British officers - Lt Col Eric Richardson and Major RH Petty - were serving with the army around 1946. Both had an interest in game-shooting and gundogs. In the American zone Major Petty had been impressed by the Weimaraners he'd seen in the hands of servicemen, and was determined to get hold of the breed come what may. Major Petty considered going into the Russian zone to meet a breeder, but that was too dangerous a mission; however, he met a breeder who had escaped from Eastern Germany, and had smuggled puppies across the border as payment for goods in short supply. It was Lt Col Richardson and Major Petty who became the founders of the breed in Britain.

Character sketch

Big and strong, the Weimaraner is intelligent and loves human company, with a tendency to be a one-person dog. He needs training from a young age and can get bored easily, so lessons should be short and interesting.

Weimaraners should be exercised until you are tired and then they can go out with another member of the family who is not tired! They need plenty to maintain their athleticism, and require things to do to maintain their mental stability.

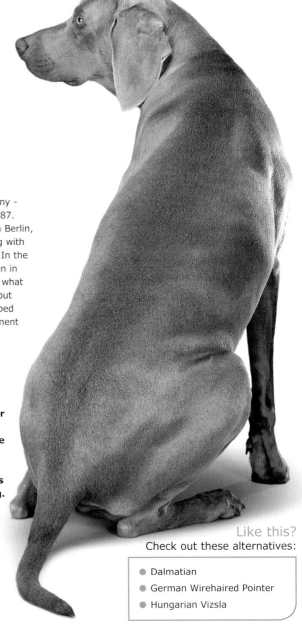

Like this?
Check out these alternatives:

- Dalmatian
- German Wirehaired Pointer
- Hungarian Vizsla

Vital statistics

Height:	56-69 cms
Weight:	25-40 kgs
Exercise:	●●●●
Grooming:	●○○○
Noise:	●●○○
Food bill:	£7.50 per week

Country of origin:	Germany
Original function:	Hunt, point and retrieve
Availability:	Moderate
Colours:	Preferably silver-grey. Shades of mouse or roe-grey permitted. The coat should give the impression of a metallic sheen
Coat type:	Short, smooth and sleek. Rarely longhaired
Coat care:	Regular brushing - daily when moulting

Health

Average life span:	11 years
Hereditary disorders:	No problems known to breeders
Hip dysplasia:	12 (breed mean score)

Suitability

Exercise:	Adult Weimaraners need a significant amount of exercise to ensure their physical and mental well-being. They are extremely energetic
Ease of training:	Moderate
Temperament with children:	Good, but kids must be taught to respect this breed
With dogs?	Okay, if not threatened
With cats?	Careful - he is a hunting dog
Town or country dog?	Country
Would he happily live in a flat or apartment?	With adequate company and exercise
Natural guard dog?	Will warn vociferously of strangers
Attitude to strangers?	Confident but reserved

Want to know more?

Breed advice: Lynne Bowley 01343 843161; Joanne Yates 07968 078112; Helena Jupp 01327 831097
Breed rescue: Jean Fairlie 01436 820478

Welsh Springer Spaniel

Character sketch

Boisterous as a young dog, the Welsh Springer is happy, faithful and devoted. He is hardy, tough and has stamina to spare.

Being very intelligent and astute, he is also easily trained. Their brains are so active that they require mental stimulation, and games should be part of their daily routine. Search and retrieve games are ideal - throw a ball and tell your Welsh Springer to find it.

A trained Welsh Springer pet is a sheer delight; they love to be with their family all the time, but don't expect a guard dog - he's far too friendly.

History

The Welsh Springer is mentioned in the Laws of Hywel Dda from the early 13th century, where it is laid down that the "spaniel of the king shall be a pound in value".

Some experts believe the Gauls migrated to South Wales in pre-Roman times, and by selective breeding of their dogs, the Welsh Spaniel was evolved. This would place the breed in Wales centuries prior to Hywel Dda's time, and so he could be described as a Celtic dog.

Though how can a dog that may well have originated in Spain arrive in Wales, when there was no communication between the two countries prior to the 10th century? One theory is that there was an early migration from Spain to Ireland, on to Wales.

Like this?
Check out these alternatives:

- Cocker Spaniel
- English Springer Spaniel
- Irish Red and White Setter

Special considerations
The Welsh Springer should not be left alone, as he gets bored very easily. He can be destructive and noisy unless adequately trained and exercised.

Vital statistics

Height:	46-48 cms
Weight:	20.5-23 kgs
Exercise:	●●●○
Grooming:	●●○○
Noise:	●●○○
Food bill:	£5 per week

Country of origin:	Wales
Original function:	Gundog
Availability:	Difficult

Colours:	Pearly white and a rich red tan
Coat type:	Flat and silky
Coat care:	Regular brushing is essential to keep the coat tangle-free and looking its best. The feathering and ears need daily attention

Health

Average life span:	13½ years
Hereditary disorders:	Eye-test parents
Hip dysplasia:	18 (breed mean score)

Suitability

Exercise:	Will take as much exercise as you can give. He needs a good daily walk, with a couple of shorter walks
Ease of training:	Moderately easy
Temperament with children:	Very good
With dogs?	Good
With cats?	Generally okay. Early socialisation is advisable
Town or country dog?	Country
Would he happily live in a flat or apartment?	Only with exercise
Natural guard dog?	No
Attitude to strangers?	Cautious but friendly

Want to know more?

Breed advice: Brenda Giles 01444 453640
Breed rescue: Heather Riley 01325 718055

Welsh Terrier

History

A Welsh poem from around 1450 describes a "black and red terrier" that hunted polecats and foxes, so some kind of terrier has existed in Wales for a very long time. But rough-coated black and tan terriers were also common in many parts of the British Isles. So which came first? In all likelihood, the modern Welsh, Lakeland, Irish, Airedale and Fox Terriers can all trace their ancestry back to these tenacious working dogs of the Middle Ages.

Illustrations from the 1800s show dogs similar to the Welsh Terrier throughout Britain. But these black and tan terriers began to decline in numbers in many parts of the country as other terrier breeds were developed. In rural, isolated areas, however, especially in north Wales, the new breeds had less of an impact.

Special considerations
Early training is essential to establish who's 'the boss'. Never let off the lead near traffic areas. Needs a good amount of exercise to keep his body and mind healthy.

Character sketch

A very energetic, happy-go-lucky dog who will happily lie on the sofa with his legs in the air and then suddenly be transformed into a hunter, fulfilling his genetic potential.

This is a real family and great house dog, with a bark much bigger than his size. He will defend you and your family should there be any threat although he is not, by nature, a noisy dog.

Feed him properly, exercise him frequently and converse with him often, and he'll become a member of your family of whom you can be proud.

Like this?
Check out these alternatives:

- Border Terrier
- Irish Terrier
- Lakeland Terrier
- Norfolk Terrier
- Norwich Terrier

Vital statistics

Height:	39 cms
Weight:	9-9.5 kgs
Exercise:	●●○○○
Grooming:	●●●○
Noise:	●●○○
Food bill:	£3.50 per week

Country of origin:	Wales
Original function:	Vermin control
Availability:	Difficult

Colours:	Black and tan, grizzle and tan
Coat type:	Wire-haired, with a solid undercoat
Coat care:	A brush and comb once or twice a week prevents tangles; hand-stripping preserves the coat's texture and colour

Health

Average life span:	14 years
Hereditary disorders:	Eye-test parents and pups
Hip dysplasia:	Insufficient numbers have been tested

Suitability

Exercise:	Regular exercise is a must. He'll take as much as you can give - and then more
Ease of training:	Moderate
Temperament with children:	Very good - if treated with respect
With dogs?	Males of the same breed can be difficult
With cats?	Okay with his 'own'; with others, take care
Town or country dog?	Country
Would he happily live in a flat or apartment?	Only with sufficient exercise
Natural guard dog?	Will guard his family faithfully
Attitude to strangers?	Not particularly suspicious

Want to know more?

Breed advice: Jo Killick 01570 470621; Susan Davison 01773 835654
Breed rescue: No known breed rescue

History

As his name suggests, the Westie is Scottish in origin. Up to about 150 years ago, the breed was a nondescript, scruffy little yard dog eking out a perilous living by killing rats and other vermin, and, at the same time, warning crofters of the arrival of intruders. As such, these dogs had no value, and there is evidence that, like so many farm dogs of the period, they were neglected and had to live on their wits.

The Westie was not a particular breed and attracted little or no attention. At the time, they probably looked mostly like a rough Cairn Terrier, coming in all colours - including white, brown, grey and black. White terriers were not in vogue, however, and were often put down at birth. It was thought, unfairly as it happens, that they were not as game or as hardy as the coloured varieties.

As fox hunting became the 'sport' of the gentry, attitudes towards dogs changed. The breeding of hounds became a fine art, and terriers came in for improvement because they were useful to the aristocrats for bolting foxes from their lairs that, in Scotland, were likely to be holes in rocks.

Character sketch

The Westie's fun-loving, devil-may-care attitude endears him to anyone who likes an active dog but wants him to live harmoniously within the family circle. He loves to run, play and explore, but will content himself with a few turns round the park if necessary.

Special considerations

Do not buy if the mother or pups have skin rashes.

Like this?

Check out these alternatives:

- Cairn Terrier
- Havanese
- Norfolk Terrier
- Scottish Terrier

Vital statistics

Height:	Approx 28 cms
Weight:	7-8 kgs
Exercise:	●●○○
Grooming:	●●●●●
Noise:	●●●○
Food bill:	About £4 per week

Country of origin:	Scotland
Original function:	Hunting and vermin control
Availability:	Easy

Colours:	White
Coat type:	Harsh outercoat with soft undercoat
Coat care:	Daily brushing is essential to keep the coat tangle-free and looking its best, in between regular professional groomings

Health

Average life span:	13½ years
Hereditary disorders:	Eye-test parents and pups. DNA test for metabolic and neurological problems
Hip dysplasia:	Insufficient numbers have been tested

Suitability

Exercise:	As much or as little as you can give
Ease of training:	Moderate. Persistent, kind training needed
Temperament with children:	Very good, if the children behave themselves
With dogs?	Generally good
With cats?	Okay with his own cats. With others - he's a terrier so watch it!
Town or country dog?	Either
Would he happily live in a flat or apartment?	Yes, but not really happily
Natural guard dog?	Very alert, will bark vociferously at intruders
Attitude to strangers?	Friendly

Want to know more?

Breed advice: Mrs W Corri 01423 770531
Breed rescue: Jan Geldart 01952 432398

Whippet

History

The Whippet was a familiar feature in many working class homes in the industrialised north of the late 19th century. These swift canines were breadwinners for poor families - they were cheap to feed and easy to house, and they earned their keep by catching rabbits for the pot.

Whippets were also often raced along narrow streets as well as on special tracks. When the Whippet first emerged as a distinct breed, they were sometimes known as snap-dogs because of their rabbit-catching skills. They were used for snap-dog coursing, which involved letting a dog loose in an enclosure full of rabbits or rats, and taking bets on the number killed. This rather brutal pastime gradually gave way to the bloodless races that are still enjoyed today.

Special considerations

The Whippet should wear a coat in the winter. It is advisable to keep clear of brambles when exercising, as the skin is thin and vulnerable.

Character sketch

This dog has a warm, affectionate nature. He is a running machine, energetic and athletic outside, with strong hunting instincts.

The breed is eminently suitable as a family pet; he counts his owners as his own pack and is remarkably loyal.

Whippets are easy to keep, having a quiet and retiring disposition when at home, and they soon suss out the softest and warmest chair. They don't eat a lot and their coat is easy to care for.

This graceful breed makes an ideal family pet. The Whippet bonds very closely with his family and has a sensitive understanding of his owner's emotions and feelings.

Like this?
Check out these alternatives:

- Afghan Hound
- Bedlington Terrier
- Borzoi
- Deerhound
- Greyhound

Vital statistics

Height:	44-51 cms
Weight:	Approx 11 kgs
Exercise:	●●○○
Grooming:	●○○○
Noise:	●○○○
Food bill:	£9 per week

Country of origin:	North Africa, but developed in Britain
Original function:	Hunting
Availability:	Easy

Colours:	Any colour or mix of colours
Coat type:	Smooth, short hair
Coat care:	A weekly brush and the occasional polish with a hound glove is all that is required

Health

Average life span:	14 years
Hereditary disorders:	No problems known to breeders
Hip dysplasia:	Insufficient numbers have been tested

Suitability

Exercise:	At least an hour's walk every day and some of that free-running
Ease of training:	Moderate
Temperament with children:	Good
With dogs?	Good
With cats?	If introduced with them as a young puppy, he should be okay; otherwise be very careful
Town or country dog?	Either, but the country is preferred
Would he happily live in a flat or apartment?	Yes, with sufficient exercise
Natural guard dog?	No, but will give a warning bark
Attitude to strangers?	Friendly

Want to know more?

Breed advice: Janice Heather 01934 733178; Elaine Day 01938 559128; Linda Jones 01234 838170
Breed rescue: Linda Jones 01234 838927

History

The Yorkshire Terrier had his beginnings in the dank, cold mines and dark mills of the northern industrial towns. Here, in the mid-nineteenth century, his purpose was to kill the disease-carrying rats that bred in their thousands and plagued the workers.

Experts today believe that Scottish terriers of various types, including the extinct Clydesdale or Paisley Terrier, had a major input into the Yorkie. It is thought that many Scottish farm labourers and miners, seeking a better standard of living, travelled south to the Leeds and Bradford area, taking their dogs with them. They wanted small terriers, so they could be carried in their pockets and taken underground or into the mills to keep down the rats.

Like this?
Check out these alternatives:

- Maltese
- Papillon
- Shih Tzu
- Tibetan Spaniel

Character sketch

One of the world's best-loved dogs, the Yorkie has great spirit and character for such a tiny dog.

Very energetic and playful, he is at his happiest when running free and hunting in the undergrowth. He is bright and intelligent, and capable of anticipating his owner's actions. He makes a good watchdog, never missing a strange noise, and he will warn of intruders, with a bark out of proportion to his size.

Special considerations
Special care should be taken of the coat if it is to be kept long.
The breed loves to play with children, but they should be taught to play gently - although Yorkies are small, they don't think they are!

Vital statistics

Height:	18-25.5 cms
Weight:	Up to 3.2 kgs
Exercise:	●●○○
Grooming:	●●●●
Noise:	●●○○
Food bill:	£4 per week

Country of origin:	England
Original function:	Ratting/companion
Availability:	Easy
Colours:	Dark steel-blue, with bright tan on chest
Coat type:	Straight, moderately long, glossy, fine and silky
Coat care:	Show coats need serious care. They are kept in crackers, and combed and conditioned regularly

Health

Average life span:	15 years
Hereditary disorders:	Parents should be eye-tested. Patella luxation
Hip dysplasia:	Insufficient numbers have been tested

Suitability

Exercise:	Garden games and a couple of walks a day should suffice. Loves free-running and play
Ease of training:	Easy, but can be stubborn. Needs firm kindness - harshness counterproductive
Temperament with children:	Very good with respectful children
With dogs?	Okay
With cats?	Okay with 'own'; be careful with others
Town or country dog?	Either
Would he happily live in a flat or apartment?	Yes
Natural guard dog?	Will warn of intruders
Attitude to strangers?	A little suspicious

Want to know more?

Breed advice: Rose Webster 01691 622332; Linda Marlow 01942 492601 or 07796 872545
Breed rescue: Beryl Evans 01234 262515

Good breeding deserves good

Read *Dogs Today* every month
Save £1.25 an issue by subscribing

The Perfect Pup was produced by *Dogs Today*, the glossy monthly magazine for everyone who loves dogs. *Dogs Today* has spent the last 19 years campaigning hard to make things better for our best friends and their owners.

Dogs Today aims to improve canine health and welfare, encourages positive training methods, and aims to bring an end to puppy farming. At the same time as being strong on campaigning for change, the magazine aims to be warm and friendly and at all times helpful and entertaining. Regular readers say it is 'like a friend dropping by each month'.

There are many interactive parts of the magazine where you can ask other readers or our experts to answer your questions. Plus we include fascinating, ground-breaking, in-depth articles with beautiful illustrations from some of the best-known and respected people in the doggie world.

We also feature celebrity dog lovers, discovering some amazing stories along the way. Recently, we had exclusive interviews with comedian Bill Bailey about his rescue dogs from Bali and we talked to *The Office* actress Lucy Davis about her good work rescuing Cocker Spaniels in LA.

reading!

MORE READING: PROMOTING BETTER **BREEDING, TRAINING** & **RESCUE**

DOGS today

September 2009
£3.75

Battery farmed yet *still* **KC reg**

We always look out for the underdog!

PLUS...
Tweet, woof! How to become a dog Twitterer!

ACTOR BILL BAILEY
He's barmy about his Bali street dogs

COMPULSION REVULSION
We back the campaign to "Ask why?" and "Say no" to bad trainers

ROTTWEILERS AS PETS
The softer side of this much-maligned breed

We also have Jemima Harrison writing for us every month - the brilliant creator of the shocking BBC documentary *Pedigree Dogs Exposed*. *Dogs Today* has always been ethical and caring and is the only dog publication involved with this pivotal documentary, which promises to bring long-overdue improvements to the future health of pedigree dogs everywhere.

To encourage you to give our magazine a go, we'd like to offer you a great subscription offer. Many of our readers admit that until they picked up *Dogs Today*, they couldn't have imagined finding a dog magazine interesting. Do give us a try!

PLUS! Don't forget that all our cover stars are selected from our readers' dogs. If you are getting a pup, do let us know and we'll see if we can squeeze you into one of our photoshoots. We use probably the best dog photographer in the world and you'll get to keep some of the photography as well as possibly seeing your dog on the cover of an international magazine! Email chloe@dogstodaymagazine.co.uk to volunteer your dog's modelling services!

Yes! I would like to subscribe to *Dogs Today* magazine

6 issues UK only for £15 - a saving of £7.50!
(see below for overseas subscriptions)

❏ Your subscription will start with the next available issue unless you tell us otherwise here: _____

Title_____ First name_____

Surname_____

Address_____

_____

_____ Postcode _____

Country _____

Contact email _____

Daytime tel no. _____

❏ Please tick if you do not wish to receive information from charities and companies who we feel may be of interest to you.

PAYMENT DETAILS:
You can also pay online at www.dogstodaymagazine.co.uk:
❏ **6 issues UK only @ £15**
❏ **6 issues including binder (UK only) @ £20**
❏ **6 issues Europe only @ £23**
❏ **6 issues Rest of World only @ £30**

I'd like to pay by cheque:
❏ I enclose a cheque/PO payable to Pet Subjects Ltd for

£_____ OR

I'd like to pay by credit/debit card:
(NB: We can only accept payment in UK currency so please use a credit card if ordering from elsewhere)

❏ **Please debit my:** ❏ Visa ❏ MasterCard ❏ Maestro ❏ Delta ❏ Amex

Card No: _____

Expiry Date: ___|___|___| Valid from: ___|___|___|

Security No: *(last 3 digits on strip on back of card)* _____

Card Issue No (Maestro only):_____

Signature: _____

Date: _____

I'd like to pay by standing order:
❏ I would like to pay £7.30 every 3 issues by Standing Order (UK only).

INSTRUCTIONS TO YOUR BANK OR BUILDING SOCIETY TO PAY BY STANDING ORDER

Account Name:_____

Account No: _____

Name of Bank: _____

Sort Code: ____   _____

Branch Address: _____

Name of organisation you are paying:	**Pet Subjects Ltd**
Sort Code:	**60-21-04**
Account No:	**36222569**
Reference No: (internal use only)	_____
Payments to be made:	**Quarterly**
Amount Details:	**£7.30**
Amount of first payment:	**£7.30**

Date of first payment_____
and on the 28th quarterly thereafter until further notice

Confirmation Signature:_____

Date: _____

POST COUPON TO: Subscriptions, *Dogs Today*, The Dog House, 4 Bonseys Lane, Chobham, Surrey GU24 8JJ OR FAX CREDIT CARD ORDERS TO: 01276 858860 OR PHONE: 01276 858880 OR EMAIL DETAILS TO: subs@dogstodaymagazine.co.uk   CODE PP01

Fido Facts at your fingertips

Got a shortlist of breeds and want to know more? Check out the list below for in-depth information on 130 different breeds. No book or other magazine gives as much in-depth, helpful information as *Dogs Today's* Fido Facts feature. For £2 per breed, we will photocopy the relevant articles from our archive and post them to you (please note that the older features will not be quite so comprehensive). We aim to send your copies out quickly, but if you are in a real hurry, or would like the feature in colour we can email a colour pdf of those breeds marked with an * to you if you supply your email address. File sizes range from 1-3mb in size, so allow 10-15 minutes for download with a 56k modem

Fido Facts Order Form

I WOULD LIKE TO ORDER THE FOLLOWING PHOTOCOPIES OR PDFS OF FIDO FACTS (TICK BREEDS REQUIRED)

Total number required _____ @ £2 each UK (£2.25 Europe; £2.50 Rest of World)

Please tick your preference between: ❏ Colour PDFs where available via email OR ❏ Black & white copies via post

- ❏ Affenpinscher*
- ❏ Afghan Hound*
- ❏ Airedale Terrier
- ❏ Akita
- ❏ Alaskan Malamute
- ❏ American Cocker Spaniel*
- ❏ Anatolian Shepherd Dog
- ❏ Australian Cattle Dog
- ❏ Australian Shepherd Dog
- ❏ Basenji
- ❏ Basset Hound*
- ❏ Beagle*
- ❏ Bearded Collie*
- ❏ Bedlington Terrier*
- ❏ Belgian Shepherd Dog*
- ❏ Bernese Mountain Dog*
- ❏ Bichon Frisé*
- ❏ Bloodhound*
- ❏ Bolognese*
- ❏ Border Collie*
- ❏ Border Terrier*
- ❏ Borzoi*
- ❏ Boston Terrier*
- ❏ Boxer*
- ❏ Briard*
- ❏ Brittany
- ❏ Bulldog
- ❏ Bullmastiff

- ❏ Bull Terrier*
- ❏ Bull Terrier (Miniature)
- ❏ Cairn Terrier*
- ❏ Cavalier King Charles Spaniel*
- ❏ Chihuahua*
- ❏ Chinese Crested
- ❏ Chow Chow
- ❏ Clumber Spaniel*
- ❏ Cocker Spaniel*
- ❏ Curly Coated Retriever
- ❏ Dachshund*
- ❏ Dalmatian*
- ❏ Dandie Dinmont
- ❏ Deerhound*
- ❏ Dobermann*
- ❏ Dogue de Bordeaux
- ❏ Elkhound
- ❏ English Setter
- ❏ English Springer Spaniel*
- ❏ Fell Terrier*
- ❏ Flat Coated Retriever*
- ❏ French Bulldog
- ❏ German Shepherd Dog
- ❏ German Shorthaired Pointer
- ❏ German Spitz*

- ❏ German Wirehaired Pointer*
- ❏ Giant Schnauzer*
- ❏ Golden Retriever*
- ❏ Gordon Setter*
- ❏ Grand Basset Griffon Vendeen
- ❏ Great Dane*
- ❏ Greyhound*
- ❏ Griffon Bruxellois*
- ❏ Hamiltonstövare
- ❏ Havanese
- ❏ Hungarian Puli
- ❏ Hungarian Vizsla*
- ❏ Irish Red and White Setter*
- ❏ Irish Setter*
- ❏ Irish Terrier*
- ❏ Irish Water Spaniel*
- ❏ Irish Wolfhound
- ❏ Italian Greyhound
- ❏ Italian Spinone*
- ❏ Japanese Shiba Inu*
- ❏ Japanese Spitz
- ❏ Keeshond*
- ❏ Kerry Blue Terrier
- ❏ King Charles Spaniel*
- ❏ Labradoodle*

- ❏ Labrador Retriever
- ❏ Large Munsterlander
- ❏ Leonberger
- ❏ Lhasa Apso
- ❏ Lowchen*
- ❏ Maltese*
- ❏ Mastiff
- ❏ Miniature Pinscher*
- ❏ Miniature Schnauzer*
- ❏ Newfoundland*
- ❏ Norfolk Terrier*
- ❏ Norwich Terrier*
- ❏ Old English Sheepdog*
- ❏ Papillon*
- ❏ Parson Russell Terrier*
- ❏ Pekingese*
- ❏ Petit Basset Griffon Vendeen
- ❏ Pharaoh Hound*
- ❏ Pointer
- ❏ Polish Lowland Sheepdog
- ❏ Pomeranian*
- ❏ Poodle (Standard)
- ❏ Poodles (Toy and Miniature)
- ❏ Portugese Podengo*
- ❏ Pug*
- ❏ Pyrenean Mountain Dog*

- ❏ Rhodesian Ridgeback
- ❏ Rottweiler*
- ❏ Rough Collie*
- ❏ St Bernard*
- ❏ Saluki
- ❏ Samoyed*
- ❏ Schipperke*
- ❏ Schnauzer*
- ❏ Scottish Terrier*
- ❏ Shar-Pei*
- ❏ Shetland Sheepdog
- ❏ Shih Tzu*
- ❏ Siberian Husky
- ❏ Soft Coated Wheaten Terrier
- ❏ Staffordshire Bull Terrier*
- ❏ Swedish Vallhund*
- ❏ Tibetan Mastiff*
- ❏ Tibetan Spaniel*
- ❏ Tibetan Terrier*
- ❏ Weimaraner*
- ❏ Welsh Corgi
- ❏ Welsh Springer Spaniel
- ❏ Welsh Terrier*
- ❏ West Highland White Terrier*
- ❏ Whippet*
- ❏ Yorkshire Terrier*

YOUR DETAILS:

Title_____

First name _____

Surname _____

Address _____

_____

_____

Postcode_____

Country _____

Daytime telephone number _____

Email address:_____

PAYMENT DETAILS

❏ I enclose a cheque/PO payable to Pet Subjects Ltd for

£_____ OR

❏ I wish to pay by credit/debit card
(NB: We can only accept payment in UK currency so please use a credit card if ordering from elsewhere)

❏ Visa   ❏ MasterCard   ❏ Maestro   ❏ Delta   ❏ Amex

Card No: _____

Expiry Date: ___|___|___| Valid from: ___|___|___|

Security No: *(last 3 digits on signature strip on back of card)*___

Card Issue No (Maestro only):_____

Signature: _____

Date: _____

❏ Please tick if you do not wish to receive information from charities and companies who we feel may be of interest to you.

PLEASE POST COMPLETED COUPON TO: Fido Facts, *Dogs Today*, The Dog House, 4 Bonseys Lane, Chobham, Surrey GU24 8JJ or if paying by credit card phone 01276 858880, fax 01276 858860 or email enquiries@dogstodaymagazine.co.uk

Plan-a-Pup - the sensible way to find your new best friend...

Are you considering getting a dog or adding to your doggie family? Would you like to know which breed or type of dog would best suit your lifestyle? Complete this form which we will send to an appropriate Plan-a-Pup advisor who will make breed recommendations for you to consider, based on your answers to this questionnaire. This is a completely free one-to-one service thanks to the generosity of our advisors.

Enclose a stamped addressed envelope and post this completed form (or a photocopy if you prefer) to: Plan-a-Pup, *Dogs Today*, The Dog House, 4 Bonseys Lane, Chobham, Surrey GU24 8JJ.

Name: _____

Address:_____

_____

_____ Postcode: _____

Email: _____

Daytime tel no: _____ Date: _____

Please tick your most accurate age band:

❏ Under 24   ❏ 25-34   ❏ 35-54   ❏ 55-64   ❏ 65-74   ❏ 75 and over

Who else lives in your house? (please give the ages of any children and explain if anyone is frail)

_____

_____

_____

_____

_____

Are you planning to have children or retire in the next 10 years?

Children   Yes ❏   No ❏

Retire   Yes ❏   No ❏

What sort of work is done by the workers in the household? Is it likely to change? _____

_____

Is there someone at home during the day? What is the maximum time the dog would be regularly left alone?

_____

_____

_____

Turn over >

Plan-a-Pup

Describe your home - is it a flat, detached, semi? Do you have very near neighbours - would a noisy dog be a problem? How big is your garden? Is it well fenced?

_____

_____

_____

_____

_____

Do you already have any dogs? Yes ❏ No ❏

If yes, how many? What sexes? Are they neutured? What breeds? What ages?

_____

_____

_____

_____

Do you have a cat? Yes ❏ No ❏

If yes, is the cat afraid of dogs? Does it run when confronted?

_____

Any other pets? Yes ❏ No ❏ (please give details) _____

_____

_____

Do you have any breeds on your shortlist? What are they and why do they appeal?

_____

_____

_____

_____

_____

_____

Have you ever owned a dog before? Yes ❏ No ❏ If yes, how long ago?_____

What breed and sex was it? _____

_____

Were you definitely the boss in the relationship or did you have any problems?
Please describe any problems _____

_____

_____

_____

Are you assertive enough for a dog to know that you're in control? Yes ❏ No ❏

Would you prefer a breed that was easy to master or are you experienced enough to tackle a breed that will need a lot of careful training? _____

_____

_____

What are you looking for in a dog? Will he need to be a guard dog as well as a companion? Would a warning bark suffice? _____

_____

_____

_____

How much exercise would you be able to give your dog every day?_____

_____

_____

_____

Are there dog friendly places to go nearby? _____

_____

_____

_____

Please tick which you would prefer:
- ❏ A walk around the block every night
- ❏ A dog who will walk for miles
- ❏ A jogging companion
- ❏ One good gallop and a walk around the block if it's raining

Would a dog that needed a lot of grooming put you off?
Yes ❏ No ❏

Would a dog that needed professional grooming be a problem?
Yes ❏ No ❏

Would a dog that shed hair be a nuisance?
Yes ❏ No ❏

Is there anybody with allergies in your household?
Yes ❏ No ❏

Would you consider an older dog from a rescue organisation?
Yes ❏ No ❏

Did you know there are specific rescues for individual breeds of dog before reading this book?
Yes ❏ No ❏

Would you be hoping to breed from your dog in the future?
Yes ❏ No ❏

Plan-a-Pup

Turn over >

Plan-a-Pup

Are you hoping to do a specific activity with your dog (eg. showing, obedience, agility, flyball etc)?   Yes ❑ No ❑

If yes, please state intended activity: _____

_____

_____

What would you be able to do to appropriately socialise your dog/puppy? _____

_____

_____

What efforts could you make to appropriately train your dog/puppy? _____

_____

_____

Can the dog be any size? Have you got a small house, car? Would food costs be a problem if you were to choose a giant breed? (please give examples - what's small to one person can be big to another!) _____

_____

_____

_____

_____

_____

Are there any breeds you particularly dislike? If so, why?

_____

_____

_____

_____

_____

_____

If your immediate household doesn't include children, do you have any that visit regularly?

_____

_____

_____

Please write any other comments you feel might be relevant to our advisor when recommending your perfect pup _____

_____

_____

_____

_____

_____